"I have traveled the world to visit sacred sites, f hold secrets light and dark. I have **never** read a better book about the history—the true history—of our most sacred of sites than Sonja Grace's *Spirit Traveler*. Sonja is a gifted researcher, author, and intuitive. Besides featuring the known history of sites including Stonehenge and St. Winefride's Well, Sonja invites us on a spirit journey. We fly with her to discover mysteries long forgotten, all of which reveal our ties to the stars and the connectivity of our souls to other people and planets. You will be fascinated, intrigued, and enlightened."
—Cyndi Dale, author of *The Subtle Body Encyclopedia*

"This densely-rendered portrait of ancient sacred sites is painted with a combination of science, history, and metaphysical research. From psychically experiencing the raw energy of Stonehenge to watching a high priestess call forth the goddess from the waters of St. Winefride's Well, Grace recounts this adventure tale of the soul with tremendous insight and a sense of wonder."
—Anna Jedrziewski, Retailing Insight

"The legends of earth temples and tombs whisper a different story of humanity. One we must listen to **now**. *Spirit Traveler* opens our hearts to new perspectives on time, reality and who we are. Theses incredible power-sites hold encrypted wisdom to show us the way to **One**. This story will inspire you to travel and know self."
—Tracey Ash, author of *Ancient Egyptian Celestial Healing*

SPIRIT
TRAVELER

UNLOCKING ANCIENT MYSTERIES
AND SECRETS OF EIGHT OF THE
WORLD'S GREAT HISTORIC SITES

SONJA GRACE

FINDHORN PRESS

ISBN 978-1-84409-694-7

Edited by Nicky Leach
Cover and interior design by Thierry Bogliolo
Artwork and maps by Sonja Grace
Printed and bound in the EU

Photo Credits:
The following photos were purchased through Shutterstock:
Tiwanaku: Gate of the Sun © Matyas Rehak
Statue at Tiwanaku © Stefano Buttafoco
Hagar Qim © Mary416
Rock of Cashel © Pierre Leclerc
Temple of Kukulcan © Sorin Colac
Great Pyramids © Kokhanchikov
Skellig Rock, Bee Hive Huts © Andreas Juergensmeier
St. Winefride's Well © Ian Taylor,
https://wellhopper.wordpress.com/2012/06/22/st-winefrides-well-holywell/
'Procession Panel', near Bluff, Utah – photo courtesy of Paul Martini

Published by
Findhorn Press
117-121 High Street,
Forres IV36 1AB,
Scotland, UK
t +44 (0)1309 690582
f +44 (0)131 777 2711
e info@findhornpress.com
www.findhornpress.com

Contents

This book is dedicated to my husband, Shawn, who is always by my side, keeping me safe and traveling the world, galaxy, and beyond with me.

Special thanks to Gail Torr, for her endless hours of editing and encouragement.

Foreword

My grandfather was solemn when he revealed the ground rules. "We never plow this field." There was a grave pallor to his face, which I recognized well from the time that he told me to always respect animals. I recall his words, "Never mistreat an animal, neither horse nor dog." He was a kindly man of the land. He knew his ground. He understood the connection to wind, rain, and sun. As we walked I felt his warmth, with my paw firmly in his hand; the age difference made us one. I was five, he closer to 75. My short legs, and his own unsteady ones, forced us to attend to each other's balance over rough, stony ground. I realized he was intentional about us walking the remnants of a famine graveyard, which straddled unkempt the lower meadow by the River Airgidín.

I liked the word ("silvery" in the old language) and would rhyme it in tune with the soft, gurgling water as it bounded our farm from McCarthy's place next door—*Arra-gudeen*. His pronouncement bore weight. I understood that there had been a great hunger in his day, and a lot of children were forced to eat grass. I had heard the awful stories from my grandmother. I liked to suck on grass stems for the sweet and acerbic juices but never ate any. The children with green lips were buried here in unmarked graves. It was hallowed ground, even if the Church didn't recognize it. On that day, I felt it to the very core of my being. I can still taste the wind, the whiff of purple heather over the empty call of the curlew. Old Tim was passing on our tribal culture, which had been just as carefully given to him nearly a century earlier. It felt heavy to now be a keeper, a holder, a teller.

The farther we become removed from the soil, the more technology we engage with, and the more distance we place between us and our farming forefathers, the more we need to reconnect with historic sites, rituals of past times, and knowledge of who we are and whence we came. Identity is a primal dust. As humans, we are bounded by our heritage, our culture, and our past. Only with surety in our own being can we set out on our solo journeys in life with confidence and zeal. Our music, our dance, our stories make us who we are, and they spring from the soil, stones, and streams. I know this because my journey has been across continents and across time. We are of the generation where the horse was replaced by the tractor, the fireside story by the radio, the radio by the television, the television by the... Well, you know where I am going with this.

Today, in my office at the university that borders the Pacific, I look across at the charts of synapses and dendrites, and I hesitate to think about the neural pathways that our new generations have outgrown. What engages our senses today are electronic ringtones, beeps, and emoticons! Gone are the sounds and sights of the iron-rimmed wheels on gravel roadways... grassy patches and ruts where the rims and clip-clop feet no longer tread. Gone are the familiar signs of morning—rooster crowing, music of milking in the cow byre—and gone to the knowledge that rain is imminent because we smell it in the clouds or the swallows are swooping lower. We have broken connections that from time immemorial were sacrosanct to our survival. What does survival look like today? Where is the nearest plug-in charge for my phone, because I do not remember phone numbers anymore?

As humans we must be rooted to our planet. We have to, or we perish. Some argue that it is already too late. Ice age? Global warming? It is of little consequence, because we are so disconnected that we do not know who to believe, who to follow, in whom to place our trust. From my boyhood I remember the stories, the connections back through the ages. I know where my ancestors came from. But there is a missing chunk, a gap. Time and memory for humans are a nebulous luxury. When I climb the rugged edge of Europe, arriving at remote beehive huts on Skellig Michael, I am connected again. I get a sense of the timelessness of existence. I know that some very smart people survived here at a time when different mindsets made sense. But questions remain. I want to know more about these people, about this site's origin, and, in particular, I want to know my connection to this space in time.

My ancestors met Patrick at the outlier geologic monolith in Cashel. It has a particular meaning for me when I walk through the ruined buildings, run my fingers over the smooth ridges of limestone that were polished by my people, and wonder at the strange Celtic crucifix that resides therein. Once again I am left with more questions than answers. Sure, there were stories and legends handed down—staff, snakes, and battles; but beyond the epic dramas, I want to know who made Cashel and why it was so important to our Celtic survival. Across the Irish Sea, which I know was at one time a land bridge to England and France, what is the reason for the remnants of ramparts, henges, and megalithic sites scattered in areas that are sometimes so remote that even sheep have difficulty hanging out there?

It is even more out of my zone of comfort to stand at the base of the Pyramids amid enduring, searing heat in Egypt, or deep in a steamy Mexican jungle at Kukulcan, and cast my mind over questions about ancient cultures, peoples, and places. Like most wicked problems, the more we know about surface geographies, elemental practices, and excavated topographies, the more questions that present themselves for deeper understanding.

I do worry about the future of the human species. This is the first time in our planetary cosmology that we are essentially urban beings, as if we have been lobotomized from feelings and a capacity for original thinking. I am not saying that the future is one of semi-robotic beings walking around with no past, no future, and no present. But I have hope. We all should. As keepers and tellers, there are messages and stories to pass on. It is our time to share our tribal knowledge with new generations. If we don't, can you imagine the newborn five generations out? What will that child have as a map? How will that young adult find his/her way in a world where no one has a history?

Spirit Travel with Sonja is one of my hope chests. I have had the pleasure of sharing physical travel in her company across the north of England, where we visited Arthur's world, Meg's world, and worlds beyond. Not only were they fascinating, pristine, and beautiful in their raw energy but they also revealed messages and past histories that connected to me in my world. Grounded in my past I am more than human; I have spirit, vision, and direction. There are so many important sites geographically dispersed across the planet that remind us that we are not alone. These sites are coherent, clear, and precise in their alignments and connections to cosmic energies, intergalactic journeys, and to times yet to come. Let the journey begin.

—**Dr. Kieran O'Mahony**, University of Washington
Author of *Parent-Teacher Potential: Connecting Neuroscience to Parenting*

Introduction

The ground on which we stand is sacred ground.
It is the dust and blood of our ancestors.
—Chief Plenty Coups, Crow (1848–1932)

Our beautiful planet, third from the sun, a gorgeous spinning globe of blue, is at least 4.5 billion years old. This massive place, with a radius of about 4,000 miles, is home to us, homo sapiens, the most intelligent species to inhabit it. In the last few hundred years, scientists have discovered how the earth was likely formed and have figured that humans first walked our planet 2.5 million years ago. Their descendants, the anatomically modern humans, appear only 200,000 years ago. While we continue to learn more about our forefathers, huge gaps in our knowledge and questions about our history still confound some of the brightest minds in the world.

Archeologists, for example, continue to puzzle over the so-called "sacred" sites that dot the earth—the pyramids, the temples, the megaliths, the statues, and the burial sites. These strange places to which humans are drawn, and where mysterious events have taken place, beg so many questions. Who built the pyramids, and where did the architects get their remarkable understanding of geometry? What was the purpose of amazing megalithic structures like Stonehenge and Tiwanaku? Were the builders master astronomers with knowledge so advanced we're only just discovering the reality of it through modern-day satellites and space telescopes? What happened at the Mayan temples, and why did the Mayans leave their beautiful structures so urgently and in ruins?

Sometimes, the answers we think we have only lead to more questions.

We know, for example, that Stonehenge was built in the Neolithic age, about 3500 BC, but it is so long ago that little evidence exists other than the stones themselves, making exact timings difficult to pin down. So while we think we can date the site's origins, the mystery surrounding how and why the site was built persists. No one can explain how the blue stones at the heart of the site, and sourced over 200 miles away, in Wales, were moved there without modern tools and technology. Debate still exists around the archeoastronomy of the site and the existence of a spiritual purpose to its alignment with the earth cycles, the stars, and the winter and summer solstices.

For what purpose was Ireland's Rock of Cashel created? Was it just a site sacred to the monks who lived there, or did it have another purpose? What about Bolivia's famous Tiwanaku? How did the site come about? Was it built where it lies, or did an earthquake move the stones? Why were the remains of headless female bodies discovered around Malta's limestone Hagar Qim? Was the site concerned with fertility rights? Archeoastronomists argue that the sacred site is linked to a pan-regional sacred geometry: Is that possible? And if so who was behind the construction? These are just some of the questions historians and archeologists still seek to answer after years of research and study.

The goal of this book is to add a new layer of knowledge to that already accumulated by the historians and archeologists. However, it's an understanding that cannot be derived from studying rock formations or digging for bones. This information cannot be gathered by just anyone; in fact, I do not know of anyone else who has the ability to reveal the secrets of the world's sacred sites as I do.

My name is Sonja Grace. I am a "spirit traveler." I travel the world in spirit form. Through meditation, I am able to defy time and space and go beyond the boundaries of the physical body. I was born with these mystical abilities, and they have been with me through every lifetime I have had here on Earth. With the aid of my guides, I have traveled to the earth's most sacred sites and discovered essential information about these mysterious places, which I share from a spiritual perspective. I have learned why they were built and what was experienced there.

In the popular television show *Outlander*, the protagonist, Claire, places her hands on the stones of an ancient megalith and time-travels to the 1700s. Her life changes completely as a result of this time-traveling experience. In essence, I suppose I am like a real-life Claire—with the ability to slip the shackles of today's time and space and travel to the beginning of these sites, then return to the present day with the knowledge of what really happened in history.

I have been a spirit traveler for over 30 years, defying time and space and putting myself in front of people who seek out my special skills and advice, wherever they are in the world. I have counseled hundreds of people from all walks of life—politicians, financiers, military personnel, professors, and celebrities. I have had many lifetimes on this planet, and in each lifetime I have experienced being a mystic or healer, which was the purpose of my first incarnation during the time of Atlantis. I am aware that I originally hail from Orion, with the purpose of bringing healing to Earth. As an ancient Orion, I have particular knowledge that allows me to spirit-travel to sacred sites around the world and implement my gifts. I frequently encounter souls that remain stuck, attached to this plane of existence, such as entities and aliens. As a healer, I am always attuned to the earth, and I respect each ancient site, the events that have taken place there, and the spirits that continue to dwell at the site.

The gift of spirit traveling is one few can claim. In profound meditation, I experience a feeling of fusion with my surroundings and a blending with everything in my space. I no longer feel a physical form. I travel with the guidance of my beloved guides, high angelic beings who assist me when I look into the ancient past.

This book describes my spirit travels to some of Earth's most famous sacred sites. For hundreds of years, people have reported sensing something about each of these sites; they have spoken of strange feelings, odd experiences. This is no surprise to me; it's no accident that these sacred sites are where they are on our planet. The goal of *Spirit Traveler* is to reveal why today's visitors often sense an air of mystery about these places. It is written with a sincere desire to add to our understanding of Earth's mysterious places. I will shed new light on recorded history and reveal new truths. My work is done with complete respect for the scientists and archeologists who have gone before. My spirit travels will reveal new stories and occurrences that weigh in where others have speculated.

I believe that, as Churchill is reputed to have said, "History is written by the victors." Historians protect particular groups or people. Politics and religion inevitably play their part in the recording of events. We're always trying to make sense of things through our modern sensibilities. We forget what people were dealing with in ancient times and, more importantly in my view, we rarely understand the incredible connectivity ancient people had with the earth. That connection is lacking today. The enduring idea is that the histories that were presented to us about these places are not legitimate.

As I spirit-travel to Stonehenge, Hagar Qim, Tiwanaku, the Temple of Kukulcan, Khafre Pyramid, the Rock of Cashel, St. Winefride's Well, and Skellig Michael, I will reveal as much as I can regarding what historians have agreed upon about the site, then reveal to you what I discovered as I traveled back through space and time to these amazing places.

For example, historians imply that Stone Age dwellers were a primitive people who spent most of their days concerned with looking for food and finding shelter. Archeologists say they had simple tools made from stone and very little else. But is this really the case? Like many of the megalithic sites, Stonehenge was built with precision, using complicated mathematical information and the kind of technology that in some cases is not even available to us today. So what are we missing? My journey though time and space will take us to meet the people who installed the stones, watch them move the stones into place, and understand why they were built. I will also describe the ceremonies performed there and provide a fresh outlook on this famous henge.

The Greeks recorded some of the first "history" of the Egyptians and based much of their reporting on sensationalism. For example, 2,000 years after Khufu built the Great Pyramid, the Greek historian Herodotus wrote what he perceived as the truth. He described Khufu's son Khafre as a tyrant with no care for the economic well-being of his community. He also reported how Khafre prostituted his own daughter. Herodotus was a reflection of his time and place in history. Certainly, what was recorded 2,000 years after the reign of Khafre is a perspective slanted to a time when Herodotus made sense of mysteries. He falls prey to the same trap as modern historians. Throughout time, humans have minimized the intelligence and abilities of people living centuries before us, often reporting speculation and exaggeration.

What part did the politics of the era play in the history of the Egyptian Great Khafre pyramid? Why was Khafre portrayed in a negative light? Why did the pharaoh Khufu and his son Khafre build these monumental emblems with methods that cannot be reproduced today? What if there were other uses for the Great Pyramids, as well as other influences far beyond the region? In my spirit travels, I have learned that there were influences the people of Egypt experienced that shaped a much different history. Many different questions arise in association with these issues: balancing the earth's poles, an unstable future, and other influences that reach far beyond our imaginations.

These will be discussed in the chapter about the Khafre Pyramid. I will explain the influence of the complicated mathematics, geometry, and astrology upon which these structures were based. This information traveled through history to freemasons, whose resulting influence had a tremendous bearing on other structures around the world.

For many people, St. Winefride's Well in Wales is a magical place with healing power. The mythic tale associated with Winefride involves her decapitation by a jilted suitor. Story has it that her head rolled downhill and where it finally stopped a fresh water spring arose. Winefride's uncle sewed her head back on. The water that he used to clean the wound was said to have magical healing power because Winefride was restored to full health. The belief in this miraculous story promoted Winefride to sainthood, and she became a part of the Church. According to local people, the well was imbued with great powers. During my spirit travel to this site, I will reveal how Winefride's love affair with a villager is the real story behind Winefride's beheading, but religious zealots of that time embellished her story to suit their needs. Historic tensions between Christianity and Paganism are important to Winefride's story, and magical powers still exist at the site today.

Skellig Michael has been thrust into the forefront of intergalactic entertainment recently because of the release of the latest installment of the *Star Wars* movie franchise. It is located in the western Atlantic, off the coast of Ireland, and is shrouded in mystery. The monastery that sits on Skellig Rock was established by a group of monks in prehistoric times. Steep stairways lead to beehive-shaped stone huts, which were erected without mortar or metal above precipitous cliffs. Built between the sixth and eighth centuries, this mysterious place has a deep spiritual history. Danger and death haunt the treacherous overhangs. My spirit travels will take me back to the time of the monks, and I will reveal what these ascetic men discovered on Skellig rock before they began to build.

In Bolivia's Tiwanaku, we explore one of the most ancient and mysterious sites in the world. Archeologists believe that the site pre-dates the Incan empire and are unsure of the early history of Tiwanaku and its people. What was Akapana Temple used for? What did the Kalasasaya, another revered structure, provide in its sacred sunken court, which has severed stone heads protruding from the interior of its sandstone perimeter walls? What was the monumental Gateway of the Sun used for, and what was the significance of the solar alignment at the single massive block of andesite? Who is the weeping figure holding a beaker in the Semi-Subterranean Temple? I will spirit-travel to this sprawling archeological site and share the secrets of who built it, what rituals were performed there, and why this magnificent city came to an abrupt end.

On the island of Malta, historians are perennially scratching their heads trying to understand the precise cut of limestone rocks that created Hagar Qim, one of the oldest recorded ceremonial sites anywhere. History records the main temple being built around 3600 BCE, but the northern ruins are considerably older. What happened here? My spirit travels will describe what these temples were built for and why there are no human bones around the site. My detailed accounting of events at the site will have you feeling as if you are there and experiencing the historic ceremonies.

The temple of Kukulcan dominates the center of Chichen Itza in the Yucatan of Mexico. The pyramid has sculptures of plumed serpents that run down the sides of the northern balustrade. During the spring and autumn equinoxes, the late afternoon sun casts a series of triangular shadows from the pyramid, creating the illusion of a feathered serpent "crawling" down the pyramid. What is the significance of the serpent during these solar cycles, and why was the Temple of Kukulcan built? What took place inside a chamber that required priests to climb 91 steps on all four sides? The sun, moon, and stars heavily influenced this sacred site, and my narrow escape in my spirit travels will reveal why.

Back in Ireland, the Rock of Cashel is also known as St. Patrick's Rock. Local folklore describes Cashel's rock as a tooth catapulted from a cave by Patrick, the fifth-century Christian missionary who was expelling the devil. Ancient energy lies beneath the rock. A round tower replaced earlier structures and continues to influence history from the 12th century to this day? Why did the king of Munster, Muircheartach Ua Briain, give the castle to the Church in AD 1101? Hold onto your hat as I take you inside the castle and reveal what the energy source is and what role the kings of Munster played in obtaining this powerful vortex of energy, which would eventually become a spiritual sanctuary.

Archeologists rely upon findings they make from artifacts excavated from sand, soil, and rocks. They interpret their findings and link them to histories that were passed down over generations. They inevitably filter their results through their historic worldview. This view of history has become accepted as true, yet many of us who visit these sites are aware of something else, perhaps another story, and another reality, that doesn't fit with what we have already been told.

I feel sure that the people who built these sacred places were far more intelligent than scientists and researchers have been able to determine. What else explains the precision of stone masonry at Tiwanaku or the Great Egyptian Pyramids? How can we account for the accuracy of astronomical alignments during the equinoxes and solstices at Stonehenge? Were our ancestors more aware of the night sky than historians have believed? It is no accident that these sacred sites are often found at high altitude, and in barren landscapes, and that their complex artistry and advanced stone masonry suggest that they were created by members of a more progressive society. More important are the sites' unseen energies—energies that I clearly perceive.

What if the small group of souls that made up the population on Earth 400,000 years ago were pioneers at the dawn of our human experience? Could it be that these souls traveled from planets within our galaxy and throughout the Universe to participate in the evolution of the human being? Is it possible that many of the first inhabitants of Earth came here as early scientists and explorers from other worlds, and does this account for the signs of a significantly higher intelligence and mathematical brilliance than we have previously appreciated? The complexity of the archeoastronomy revealed in the planned structures that mark the passage of the sun and moon at some of these sites tells of knowledge so advanced that it still baffles today's scientists. Just how smart was mankind 8,500 years ago? Did star beings walk the earth and build these sacred places? What is the function of these sacred sites on the earth and beyond into the Universe? Are these sites linked in ways we don't yet understand?

The many lifetimes our souls have spent here on Earth, I believe, explains why we often feel a connection with a particular historical site. Some of us feel an intense sense that we've been to the site before or "know" something about it. It is possible that we were connected to these sites in previous lives. Our ancestors understood the interconnectedness of our souls and were fully aware of the star beings that gifted them the technology and awareness to create these sites. Furthermore, our ancestors revered them and made them gods. They told stories about these gods and goddesses and celebrated them by creating art, statues, buildings, and all kinds of artifacts around these sites. Generations later, we are trying to decode and decipher the clues they left behind. The Great Pyramids, Tiwanaku, and Hagar Qim are not just piles of old rocks; they speak of a people from long ago who worshipped the sun, the moon, the stars, and the planets and each and every one of the souls that inhabit them.

The ancient science of astronomy (archeoastronomy) guided our predecessors to inhabit particular places on Earth. In addition, they directed them to harness the energies of the annual solstices and equinoxes with extraordinary accuracy.

I believe that the Universe has no boundary and is teaming with life. We are only just beginning to learn about the historic interplay between humans on this planet and these other life forms. I will show through my spirit travels that each of these sites tells of visitations from star beings. They divined their environment with a completely different system and sensory perception. I am grateful for the privilege of taking you there to reveal those extraordinary beings and events.

*History is simply a series of events that are completely
generated from karma or emotional wounds that become
a vibration that everyone feels and responds to.*
—Sonja Grace

1

Stonehenge

*Much of what has been written about Stonehenge is
derivative, second-rate or plain wrong.*
—Christopher Chippindale, *Stonehenge Complete*, 1983

One of the most treasured prehistoric monuments in the United Kingdom is Stonehenge. It is an ancient round of stones surrounded by Neolithic and Bronze Age monuments. Stonehenge is located in Wiltshire, England, and there are constant discoveries and new speculations as to why it was built.

British prehistory has very few records of Stonehenge's construction, but the oldest remnants at the site are the pine posts found near the monument. Scientists have carbon-dated these and found that they are around 10,500 years old. Current archeological thinking shows a pattern of development over a period of approximately 10,000 years at the site.

The first excavation of Stonehenge took place in the 17th century by the Duke of Buckingham, prompted by a visit from King James I, sometime in the 1620s. King James subsequently commissioned the celebrated architect Inigo Jones to conduct a survey and study of the monument. Jones argued that the Romans built Stonehenge.[1]

King James asked Inigo Jones to produce an accurate plan and description of Stonehenge. Interestingly, the site featured as an important war monument in Arthurian legend, and King James was keen to prove that he was connected to King Arthur.

Since this first report, in the 1650s, there have been hundreds of major historical investigations into Stonehenge over several centuries, and there are thousands of books and scholarly texts on the subject. Over the years, these investigations have uncovered a lot of valuable information about the development of Stonehenge. Most of these studies have been based on a belief that people of that time were hunter-gatherers living in a simple world. The various sites surrounding Stonehenge, such as the burial mounds, have also garnered much speculation as to the builder and their purpose.

Construction

The first identifiable phase of construction at Stonehenge was a simple circular structure built around 5,000 years ago. However, it is believed that the site had spiritual importance long before that. A foundation was dug out using deer bones and antlers, along with a ring of 56 circular pits (named

Aubrey Holes), possibly to hold timber posts. There appears to have been a second phase of building, defined by the arrival of the so-called "blue stones," volcanic rocks found in Wales. Radiocarbon dating of the stones, carried out in 2008, suggests that the first stones were raised between 2400 and 2200 BCE.[2] Mystery surrounds how these stones, which weighed over 5 tons, were transported to the site. Historians speculate that the ancients used the River Avon as a means of transportation; however, the exact means by which they were transferred to the site is unclear.

Scholars think that once the blue stones were erected, they only stood for about a century before being repositioned as part of what current archeological thinking calls the third phase of building. Thirty new and massive stones were transported from about 20 miles (32 kilometers) away. They were 10 feet (3 meters) tall and weighed over 27 tons. Known as the Sarsen Stones, they were placed in the previously dug-out ditch and topped with 30 lintels using a crude form of joinery.

The next structure built as part of this phase was the Trilithon Horse Shoe. It is a group of five stones built in the shape of a horseshoe. Another set of structures was also built and was made up of two stones with a lintel on top. It is called the Trilithon set. There are several of them, and they are ordered according to their size. The Trilithon Stones weigh 50 tons and are topped by 10-ton lintels.

The next phase of building involved the raising of the Station Stones and the digging of ditches, called burial barrows, which surround them. The Slaughter Stone is at the entrance to the site and runs parallel to another set of ditches. The Heel Stone, which leans, is thought to have once been part of a pair of stones and can be found at the side of the ditches. One other notable stone is the giant sandstone Altar Stone, which can be found at the center of the Trilithon Horseshoe. The final phase of building at Stonehenge was completed about 3,500 years ago.

Purpose

Several theories exist as to the purpose of the site—ceremonial, funerary, archeoastronomy, or perhaps something else. Evidence suggests that the site may have been used as a burial site during parts of its history. Cremated remains were found in the Aubrey Holes, and more remains were found in the ditches, indicating that the site was funerary from the outset. Randolph E. Schmid reports the cremated remains continued to be deposited for 500 years at least. Some of the remains found at the site could be dated back as far as 3000 BCE.[3]

Other historians believe that Stonehenge was built for ceremonial purposes, as a place of worship by the ancient people who built it. It may have been a place to celebrate the sun or moon gods. Scholars know that the Druids used the site, although they didn't build it.

Builders

While no one has proven emphatically who built the monument, historians have concluded that three tribes built Stonehenge over the three distinct periods outlined above. The ancient people of 5,000 years ago survived off the land, eating what they could hunt and grow. This group of people is identified as the Neolithic agrarians, and they were semi-nomadic. They raised cattle, sheep, goats, and pigs, and they are thought to have treasured circles and symmetry. They lived in tribal groups and were clan-based, much like indigenous people around the world. They had responsibilities to their clan and their tribe and to the spiritual hierarchy, and are believed to have been responsible for the first phase of building. They created furrows and mounds in a circular shape or on the hilltops, where they buried their people in an east-west direction and entombed them with large stones. (The Hopi bury their dead in the same way in the southwestern United States.)

Archeologists have determined that the Neolithic structure was built during the same time as Newgrange in Ireland. Both of these sites are related to the sun and moon cycles. At Stonehenge, the principal axis of the Sarsen structure is aligned with the midsummer solstice sunrise.[4]

The next set of builders came from the plains of Europe and invaded the area around Stonehenge 4,000 years ago. Known as the Beaker Folk, their name comes from the strange-looking cups, made from clay, found buried with their dead. Rather than create mass burial tombs, the Beakers dug out small, round graves, which they then topped with a mound of earth. Along with the strange-looking pot cups, archeologists found battle axes, daggers, and other objects, suggesting they were warlike aggressors. Historians think the Beakers were hard working and lived communally, organized around a chieftain system. They appear to have used complicated mathematical concepts and, like those before them, worshipped the sun.

*When any work seems to have required immense force
and labor to effect it, the idea is grand. Stonehenge,
neither for disposition nor ornament, has anything admirable;
but those huge rude masses of stone, set on end,
and piled each on other, turn the mind on the
immense force necessary for such a work.
Nay, the rudeness of the work increases this cause of grandeur,
as it excludes the idea of art and contrivance;
for dexterity produces another sort of effect,
which is different enough from this.*
—Edmund Burke 1729–1797

The Wessex people are credited with the final phase of building. They were an advanced culture, organized tribally and were skilled traders. This was during the Bronze Age, around 3,500 years ago, and archeologists think that these people inscribed the bronze dagger carving that can be seen on one of the large Sarsen stones. The Wessex people were wealthy and smart; they built with precision, using complicated calculations and advanced construction techniques.

Scientists and historians have unearthed much about Stonehenge that informs our understanding of the people who built it. But it is clear that there are all sorts of questions about how these ancient people were able to create what they did. It is impossible to imagine the Neolithic Agrarians, the Beaker Folk, or the Wessex People building Stonehenge without a great deal of help.

According to *Science and Stonehenge: Proceedings of The British Academy*, edited by renowned archeologists Barry Cunliffe and Colin Renfrew (The British Academy, 1997), the principal figure in the major excavations at Stonehenge between 1950 and 1964 was Professor Richard Atkinson. In his book, *Stonehenge* (Pelican, 1960)[5], Atkinson gave a vivid account of what was then the prevailing view regarding the Wessex People who built Stonehenge:

*And yet were these Wessex chieftains alone responsible for the
design and construction of this last and greatest monument at
Stonehenge? For all the evidence of their power and wealth,
and for all of their widespread commercial contacts, these men*

were essentially barbarians. As such, can they have
encompassed unaided a monument which uniquely transcends
all other comparable prehistoric buildings in Britain and indeed
in all Europe north of the Alps, and exhibit so many refinements
of conception and technique? [...] I for one do not believe it.
Is it then any more incredible that the architect of Stonehenge
should himself have been a Mycenaean than that the monument
should have been designed and erected, with all its unique and
sophisticated detail, by mere barbarians?

Colin Renfrew disagreed with Professor Atkinson's assumptions. He refuted any possibility that Stonehenge was built by the Mycenaeans. In 1995, he was proved to be correct when high-precision radiocarbon dating showed Stonehenge to be much, much older than Mycenae.

The problem of course remains, as Professor Atkinson pointed out, that it seems highly unlikely that a group of Stone Age barbarians from ancient Britain had the kind of construction knowledge and sophistication to have been the masterminds behind Stonehenge. Some scholars have looked to ancient Egypt for answers. Again though, this seems to be unlikely, and historians now know that construction at Stonehenge began many years before the building of the Great Pyramids. Consequently, the question still hangs in the air like a dense fog: Who built Stonehenge?

There is a feeling of recognition, as of meeting an old friend,
which comes to us all in the face of great artistic experiences.
I had the same experience when I first heard an English
folksong, when I first saw Michelangelo's Day and Night,
when I suddenly came upon Stonehenge or had my first sight of
New York City—the intuition that I had been there already.
—Ralph Vaughan Williams, composer, 1872–1958

The creation of Stonehenge boggles the mind. On an energetic level, it represents centuries of human experiences that we can feel through our senses, while the grandeur of this monument dwarfs even the greatest cathedrals in the world. One can imagine the impression of this megalithic structure and how it might have been shared in the folklore of the time. Among the many myths and legends about the site are that giants moved the stones to this location, witches held rituals at the site, Romans built the monument, and the Druids practiced ancient magic there. Historians and those that record history are always influenced by the time in which they write. Even Professor Atkinson, an academic, was moved by what he felt there. This site carries a feeling that is undeniably charged with energy that most people can feel.

The Mystery of Salisbury Plain

The land around Salisbury Plain, the location of Stonehenge, is shrouded in mystery. The energy of this vast land is quite different in both look and feel. It makes you wonder what happened on Salisbury Plain that such a monument was erected in that very spot. Why there?

Could we be asking the wrong questions? Is it that something happened there long before the monument was even built? Perhaps the people practiced ceremonies that, as in any culture, morph and change over time. How did the people of each century adapt and use this site in ways that varied from the one before? Could it be that the many stone circles throughout Britain, which have been reconstructed over time, were simply markers of what the people of the time felt? Were the sites portals of energy?

It is possible that these sites, which are all circular in shape, represent a much greater symbol: the circle of life. Many megalithic sites also possess spiral mounds, which is possibly an ancient symbol for the Universe and is significant throughout the region. Most researchers agree that these people worshipped the sun, moon, and stars. Another possible reason for the abundance of circular shapes at these sites is the representation of the womb. Our ancestors were significantly more connected to the cycle of life than we are. They lived close to the earth, they heard and saw all of nature, and their artwork and artifacts reflect this direct communication with Source.

Adding to the mysteries surrounding the site are the stories that exist in folklore. For example, there is a legend of a war between the Britons and Saxons around AD 450, which took place on the Salisbury Plain. It is believed that the Saxons killed 460 British noblemen. Aureoles Ambrosias, king of the region, ordered Ireland's Giant Ring Circle be moved to the site as a memorial to the British soldiers who had died. The king sent his brother, Uther Pendragon, to transport the circle from Ireland. A massive army of 15,000 men was unable to move the stones, given their enormous size and weight. The legend goes on to tell how Merlin arrived with his magical powers, and all of the stones were moved to their place.

Another story tells of an old Irish woman who has constructed Stonehenge in her backyard. This ancient tale reflects the beliefs of the times. The Devil is said to have wanted the stones for himself, so, disguised as a gentleman, he visits the old woman. He asks her if the stones are for sale. She does not want to part with the stones. However, the Devil is carrying a large bag of money and strikes a deal with her. The Devil allows the old woman to keep what she can count of his money in the time it takes him to move the stones. She only agrees to this because she believes the Devil is a gentleman and assumes it will take him a very long time to move the stones.

Of course, she doesn't have a chance to count any coins because the Devil moves the stones with his powers. He brags later that no one will ever know the exact number of stones at Stonehenge. But the legend goes on to describe how a wise friar guesses the number of stones correctly, and as a result, the angry devil throws one of the stones at him. The friar is hit in the heel, causing a dent in the stone. Today, this stone is known as the Heel Stone at Stonehenge.

Mathematics and Geometry

Another source of mystery and clues about Stonehenge can be found in the mathematics and geometry of the site. There is far too much complicated geometrical information for me to go into all of it but, briefly, here are some of the most salient facts.

Anyone who has researched the site recognizes that its construction embodies the elegant and universal symbolism of numbers and geometry. There are all sorts of geometrical relationships that can be drawn between the squares and the circles. The Neolithic builders, if that's who they were, accurately created polygons, which included hexagons, pentagons, and decagons. The position of the stones in the Sarsen circle is a classic 30-sided figure (a triacontagon). Furthermore, the horseshoe form of the central array was derived from the same markers that determined the position of the Sarsen Circle.

Beyond the circle, the four Station Stones sit in perfect spatial and geometric relationship with the central group. The focus on the archeoastronomy of the site, and its alignments with the sun and moon, has tended to distract attention away from the simple elegant geometrical formulae used by its prehistoric designers.

Perhaps one of the most interesting items discovered at the Stonehenge complex is not the stones themselves but the Bush Barrow Lozenge, an artifact found at the Barrow site, nearly a kilometer away from the stones themselves. Found in one of the graves, it is probably an item of jewelry and is made of pure gold. Most interesting, though, is its design. It contains repeating hexagons and circles that have been executed with such accuracy and precision that it raises all sorts of questions about the craftsmen behind it. As Anthony Johnson notes in his book *Solving Stonehenge*:[6]

> The Bush Barrow Lozenge (buried c.1700 BC; the exact date of its manufacture is unknown) is one of a number of objects that provide a further remarkable insight into the sublime dimension of the prehistoric mind. This artefact is a tangible and intimate connection with the creativity of the Early Bronze Age artisans, a mature reflection of the geometric principles developed not by "astronomer priests" but by Neolithic "draftsmen-surveyors" who had used the same elegantly simple methods in the construction of both timber and stone monuments for generations.

Archeoastronomy

Of course much has been written about the archeoastronomy of Stonehenge, and indeed, it is one of the most fascinating aspects of the site. It is obvious to those who have studied Stonehenge that particular significance has been given to the annual solstices and equinoxes. The summer solstice sun rises close to the Heel Stone, and the sun's first rays shine into the center of the monument between the horseshoe-shaped stones. While it is possible that such an alignment could be coincidental, this astronomical orientation had been acknowledged since William Stukeley drew the site in 1720 and first identified its axis along the midsummer sunrise.

Stukeley noticed that the Heel Stone was not precisely aligned on the sunrise, even though, year to year, the movement of the sun across the sky appears to be regular. The axis of the earth has shifted—earthquakes, in particular, have had an impact on ecliptic illuminations at sites all around the world. Creating the Heel Stone alignment may have also been more difficult thousands of years ago, which could be another reason for the slight inaccuracy.

Stukeley and the renowned astronomer Edmund Halley showed that any magnetic compass the builders used to lay out the site would have likely varied from true north quite a bit.

In 1963, British-born astronomer Gerald Hawkins used a computer to calculate the eclipses and argued that Stonehenge was probably used to predict eclipses. I think there is no doubt that Stonehenge was built with the sun in mind and to align the monument with the solstices. Aligned with the River Avon, the avenue connects the monument to the winter solstice. The site faces the summer solstice sunrise, and through the intricacy of this mathematical masterpiece, we can observe that not only did the sun, moon, and stars relate to this site but so did the universal symbolism of numbers and geometry.

Death

Stonehenge is also mysteriously connected to death, dying, and funerals. Burial pits are found at the site and around this megalithic complex as well as at other stone circle sites in Britain. According to archeologists, the first phase at Stonehenge was a simple circular structure around 2900 BC in the Neolithic landscape. Burial mounds (long barrows) were the local centers for scattered communities, and so-called "causewayed camps" were the regional centers for meetings and rituals associated with burial.

Historians speculate that the elite of these ancient communities were buried in the mounds near the monument; for this reason, they have focused on these burial sites as the key reason Stonehenge exists. But what if this site were a portal? What if viewing this from the air gave it a whole new meaning?

In the Middle Ages, Stonehenge was known as *Chorea Giganteum*, or the Giant's Dance, a reference to the oral history of this monument, which includes stories of giants who placed the stones here and magical beings seen throughout history. So the question archeologists have pondered is: Was Stonehenge used for astronomical events beyond the midsummer and midwinter solstices? The answer is yes!

Aerial Perspective

Other researchers have pointed to the aerial mystery of Stonehenge and the possibility that the stones represent something from an aerial perspective. Much as we observe crop circles from the air, and sit in awe of the intricate design of each pattern that is carved out in a farmer's field, we might have the same experience from the air, as we look down on 56 stones surrounded by 30 sarsen stones, which together make a giant mathematical equation that even scientists today struggle to understand.

Nearby, the Woodhenge, an octagon shape, and two rectangular shapes grace Salisbury Plain. When you look at it from an aerial point of view, it resembles a clock—the octagon shape is the sun, or the center; Stonehenge is at six o'clock; Woodhenge is at 3 o'clock; and the rectangles are at 12 o'clock and 9 o'clock. You would not know this unless you observed it from the air. As a landscape, Salisbury Plain in its entirety is a big part of why this megalithic site was built here.

Sound Frequency

The ancient engineers also knew something about sound frequency. Rarely mentioned is the mystery of the acoustics at Stonehenge. Steven Waller, a researcher in archeoacoustics, has a theory that circular constructions like this one were created to mimic a sound illusion. He claims that the listener would notice a strange effect if two pipers played instruments standing on either side of Salisbury Plain—the dual pipes would cancel each other out, with the sound waves literally creating quiet spots.

In 2012, Waller reported to the American Association for the Advancement of Science that the stones of Stonehenge create a similar effect. Rather than creating competing sound waves, the stones block sound. Legends associated with Stonehenge also reference pipers, Waller said, and prehistoric circles are traditionally known as "piper stones." Waller's theory is speculative, but other researchers have confirmed that Stonehenge had amazing acoustics. A study released in May 2012 found that the circle would have caused sound reverberations similar to those in a modern-day cathedral or concert hall.[7]

With all these mysteries about Stonehenge still unsolved, we're no closer to answering the questions about why the site was built. Was it for religious purposes; ceremonial practices; to aid healing; as a pilgrimage site; for sun, moon, sky, and earth worship; or as an astronomical marker? Are we ready to learn what really happened in the past beyond the confines of our own dogma and beliefs? Perhaps, in time, scholars will determine the answers to some of the mysteries of Stonehenge.

In my spirit travels from my home in Oregon, I have had the opportunity to experience something I am sure most scholars would give their eye teeth for. My experience of Stonehenge, and why it was created and what it was used for, will be described in the next section.

Spirit Traveling
to Stonehenge

When I woke on the morning of my first spirit travel to Stonehenge, I had an odd feeling. My dreams the night before had been filled with images of stones and voices of the past. I went about my usual routine, and sat down in meditation with a feeling of anticipation.

As I closed my eyes I kept seeing my guides standing in front of me, waiting. I traveled into a deep state of peace, while my guides stood there waiting, holding out their hands. It was an invitation to travel. Excitement raced through me.

I was instantly weightless, and the earth disappeared beneath me. In seconds, I was airborne, traveling through the atmosphere, completely unaware of time. All I knew was to hang onto the hand of my guide. Before long, we pushed through a cloudy mass and descended to the grassy field below. There was a cold gentle breeze moving my hair and clothes. I felt cold and wrapped my sweater around me tightly. There appeared to be people around me, but I knew from their transparency that these figures were not fully formed humans. They were spirits—the ghosts of those whose lives had ended on Salisbury Plain.

The area was filled with a glowing and warm light. It was like the sun at dawn, but it was clearly not the sun. Still holding my hands, my guides ushered me toward the giant stones that loomed over us. Immediately, I felt the presence of the stones. The hair on my arms tingled, and goosebumps covered my body. The giant stones were alive with an energy infused from the past.

I looked around and saw that I was standing right in the middle of the ancient ruin. The guides told me they were going to show me the beginning of this ancient site, why it was created, and what the people practiced. Suddenly, it was as if the air pressure around me had changed, and without even blinking, I was transported back through time. I found myself standing on the same ground, only now it was bare and without stones, just grass and dirt. I could smell the earth and feel the crisp clean air in my nose.

I was aware of an energy that was pulsing through the very site we were standing in. I could feel a powerful vibration rising through my feet and a wave of celestial energy flowing through my head and body. I understood that the stones held the energy of the site but that a new awareness was about to be revealed. There had been much more going on in this place before the stones were ever placed at Stonehenge.

I turned to look at my guides, who were illuminated by a light from within. As they spoke, they moved their hands to show me that before these megalithic standing stones had been placed on Salisbury Plain, there were layers upon layers of markers identifying the site. The land at the beginning was bare and contained a raw and intense energy. This portal energy would develop and intensify over centuries and capture the attention of humanity. I could feel it in this moment—the energy was moving from the earth upward and from the sky downward. I felt I was in a whirlpool of cosmic proportions.

Gradually I sensed the earth had stopped moving. Kneeling on the ground, I slowly lifted my eyes. It was brighter. Right before me stood tall luminescent beings. They were not my guides. One of them spoke to me in a deep voice, identifying who they were. They were from the star constellation of Pleiades (I call them the Ancient Ones). They had arrived to share with me the early history of this site known as Stonehenge.

The Ancient Ones had a great deal of influence on the human race. In 10,000 BCE, after the last ice age, four portals opened here, bringing the celestial energy needed to restructure life on Earth.

At this time, Earth was in the second realm of consciousness and in the beginning of the fourth dimension. Lumeria was an ancient civilization off the west coast of Ireland. It had just come to an end. Atlantis, another ancient civilization, off the coast of Africa, had also come to an end. Atlantis was a large landmass once attached to Morocco and the Canary Islands. It had moved south under Antarctica. Both Lumeria and Atlantis ended with the complete disappearance of their large and advanced civilizations.

My attention moved to the voice of a woman who stepped forward and continued to explain why Salisbury Plain was part of a much bigger portal. The world's continents had shifted and were in the process of recovering from those catastrophic tectonic movements. Only small groups of humans survived, she explained. These kinds of continental shifts have taken place many times over the billions of years of this planet's existence. Each time plates move and land masses shift, there is an equal shift in planetary energy. She pointed skyward and explained that energy is often coming in from the cosmos. These cosmic rays have a direct impact on Earth. Suddenly, I felt her communicating with me telepathically. She acknowledged my thought that to this day science does not know the exact effect cosmic rays have on Earth.

The male voice came back to the front again, where the Ancient Ones stood, and told me that the portal covered all of the United Kingdom 12,000 years ago. Three other portals were equal in size to this one: one in China, one in Central America, and one in Egypt. The energies that came to Earth helped the planet to prepare for the next phase. He explained that Earth and all of its inhabitants have what they call "phases" that are roughly 30,000 years long.

I realized that the Ancient Ones were no longer moving their mouths to speak to me, and that we were now telepathically connected. They shared information about their passage to Earth along a fantastic superhighway from the cosmos. I could see that it was part of a hologram located at Castlerigg, another stone circle, in northern England's Lake District.

This bridge between the cosmos and Earth is energetic in nature but quite real in ways humans have not understood. Intricate silver and gold line its outside edges, and a vast array of colors is woven together to form a solid path illuminated by its own energy. It stretches to the center of the galaxy. From there, a network of subsequent bridges span the Universe. The energy bridge at Castlerigg was open at the dawn of Earth's existence and continues to open at each new phase. This energy superhighway reaches into our galaxy to signal other life forms. Higher intelligence understands what this bridge is for and recognizes when a new phase is beginning on Earth.

The female voice spoke once again, explaining that throughout our galaxy and beyond are soul groups known as "demi-gods." Much larger than humans, they stand about 12 feet (3.7 meters) tall. These demi-gods have human features indicative of where they are from. She described the different demi-gods, ranging from Ra and Sekhmet to Vishnu and Krishna, Thor and Oden, and many more. These demi-gods participated in the evolution of humans from 8000 BCE onward. Humans around the world were influenced both culturally and physically by the many different celestial beings. The Tibetan gods shaped the human population of China, and the Egyptian gods created a rich culture on the African continent but at the same time enslaved many of the humans. The tall slender stature of the Egyptians resembled Ra and Hathor. In Mesoamerica, the Hopi gods influenced the people.

The Norse gods of the Northern European landmass left a strong impression on the way Britons and people of Norway, Sweden, Denmark, and France looked, despite the fact that the Ancient Ones were also involved there. Physically, the people of Northern Europe have a stature that reflects the

Norse gods, but mentally and spiritually, they are clearly descendants of the Ancient Ones.

The Ancient One went on to show me how the demi-gods are influenced by the energies of the planet they come from, which is in turn reflected in their physicality. The demi-gods can manifest as solid figures or remain luminescent. Demi-gods have evolved the human race in every way, and since the beginning of time.

The Beginning

A new voice broke the silence, and when I looked up I saw another male stepping forward. His hair was like spun gold and his voice clear and direct. The Ancient One insisted that their purpose on Earth has always been to help develop the human race. Through their technology, which far surpasses anything we understand even today, they have constantly given humans the tools with which they could better understand their world and, ultimately, the higher intelligence that created it.

Since the last ice age, Stonehenge has been a sacred place. In the beginning, the Ancient Ones visited four times a year, to mark the two solstices and two equinoxes. The visits continued at the vernal calendar each spring. As each age brought in a new awareness, their visits became less frequent in hopes of humanity reaching their potential.

The Ancient Ones began to move together, and the one with the gold-spun hair motioned for me to step closer. As I moved toward him, he explained how the use of the land on Salisbury Plain had changed throughout history, depending upon the most prominent belief system and sociological structure. Each century brought change. In the beginning, all you would have seen at this site was naked ground adorned with small branches and stones. Later, a wooden arbor spanned the entire site, and later still, the large Sarsen Stones and Blue Stones became the prominent features.

With each improvement and physical change at the site that we now call Stonehenge came an evolving humanity. The Ancient Ones understood the basic nature of humanity, including its flaws, wide spectrum of emotions, and strong need to survive. With each visit, the Ancient Ones educated the people. They taught them how to use the land and harness the energy that came from this portal. The site took on different appearances that would later cause great confusion for historians.

I became conscious of the Ancient One who was giving me all this information. He was leading me around Stonehenge, and we were floating as we observed the different layers of time. Magically, he moved his hand and, suddenly, the sight before me changed from ground covered with small rocks and branches to the wooden arbor and then massive stones. I witnessed the destruction of the arbor by invaders and the conflicts that took place on Salisbury Plain. I even watched as the Sarsen Stones and Blue Stones levitated into place.

He moved his hand again, and we were peering into the earth, where he showed me the layers of history and stones that lie deep underground. He said more stones were placed around 5200 BC and that the stones that stand today were placed around 4000 BC. This was the last time the Ancient Ones visited Salisbury Plain. These stones were placed to remind humans of the presence of the Ancient Ones and all they had learned from them.

What happened next was one of the most intimate exchanges I have had with the earth to date. The Ancient One drew me near the large Sarsen Stone and told me to listen. I put my ear next to the giant and could hear the voice of the stone. This grand megalith was sad and filled with memories of the past. I listened as the spirit of the rock told me how each one of the stones had held the energy of the portal and kept it open. Over time, they lost their power due to an increase in misuse of the site. As I turned to look at the Ancient One for confirmation of what I had just heard, he told me that sacrifice and bloodshed had eventually brought the portal to a close.

Life and Death

I stepped back a few paces. I realized I was standing in a circle made by the stones and shaped like the letter C. At the opening of the C shape is a causeway. Clearly, this represents the impregnation of the people. It's a phallic symbol, and the circle is the womb.

The female Ancient One came forward and with a nod acknowledged telepathically that I was indeed correct. Stonehenge was the site where the Ancient Ones and humans procreated. Then she explained their genetic influence on the human race. She told me that the Ancient Ones brought life to the people through procreation and ceremony. They multiplied and developed into a new and more advanced race of humans. However, human understanding during this period was limited to the worship of the demi-gods. Worship took the form of ceremonial practice.

The humans living in 4000 BCE understood that when the Blue Stones and large Sarsen Stones were placed, the Ancient Ones were not coming back. They had been told this since the beginning of the new phase. The humans had relied on the Ancient Ones for centuries, and the next thousand years would lead to a growing separation anxiety. The humans kept and added to their ceremonies and rituals. The additions reflected the symbolic events and were based on the constellations and placement of the stars. Ultimately, the goal was to bring back the Ancient Ones, and they resorted to sacrificial rituals in which animals were killed as a way of appealing to the demi-gods to return.

The female leaned closer and, looking deep into my eyes, communicated that the gods never wanted human sacrifice but that people simply fell into fear and anxiety once the Ancient Ones left. By 3000 BCE, the human belief system had morphed into one of total separation. They began to bury the high priestesses near the portal, so they would have access to the Ancient Ones. Their view of the afterlife was mixed with the teachings of the demi-gods and superstition caused by famine and war.

For more than two thousand years, it became important to be buried next to the site, which was considered a direct line to the demi-gods and the afterlife. She said the legends of the demi-gods eventually faded, and new stories emerged about the Norse gods. As wars raged, the influence of the Norse gods grew. The original ceremonies and teachings of the Ancient Ones began to disappear or become mixed up with new forms of celebration and ritual.

The Ceremony

The Ancient Ones revealed the first ceremony performed at this sacred earth site. The landscape transformed to the original bare ground, with only small stones and branches identifying the portal. Male demi-gods and female humans were participants in a ceremony unfolding before me. They moved in reverential silence down a causeway, entering the portal and taking up positions where the Sarsen Stones stand today. The stars sped around the bright night sky to find their particular position on this night back in 8000 BCE.

I felt humbled as I watched what no one else had previously seen. The females paired with the Ancient Ones, until 14 couples filled the inner circle, awaiting the energy of the portal to intensify and become visible to the naked eye. Energy streams of gold-and-white light came pouring down from the heavens, while a blue hue rose from the earth. The couples moved to openings in the outer circle marked with smaller stones and defined by branches so that the circle looked like flowers. They closed their eyes, and the energy of the portal reached new heights. A wave pushed down on my head, while others rose up through my feet. Clear-crystal energy descended through the portal, lighting up the circle and filling my body.

The couples moved into the womblike openings and lay upon the earth, their heads facing toward the center and their legs pointing outward like spokes on a wheel. A warm breeze moved through the circle. The fertility rights began. A profound union was taking place, one marked with love and tenderness and the intent of bringing forth a star child. The space between the stones in which the couples laid was symbolic of the pathway to the Pleiades, from which the Ancient Ones had come. The women received the energy coming from the portal through the top of the head and down through their body. The demi-gods received this cosmic energy through their feet, traveling upward, where it delivered a star seed into the woman.

Finally the couples rose from the ground and walked in a spiral formation, symbolizing the movement of the Universe. (This symbol is found on ancient sites around the world.) Once the women carrying the star seed reached the altar, the Ancient Ones washed them in honor, using mint and other evergreens. Then they left the circle together, walking solemnly back down the causeway.

The Ancient Ones smiled telepathically, acknowledging what I knew to be true—that the human race was created with the help of the demi-gods. Few women were selected for this great honor, and those bearing a star child became high priestesses and were consulted as spiritual leaders. As high priestesses they were in charge of all ceremonies at Stonehenge for the next 4,000 years.

This particular ritual evolved as more children were born of the Pleiadian race. In 3000 BCE, the ceremonies practiced at Stonehenge morphed once again, when the Druids used the site. This time, it was men not the high priestesses of ancient times who influenced these rituals. They would make this fertility ceremony their own. They also created a spring ritual with the same intention. The Druid men felt they must divine the demi-gods and bring them through their own physicality. They used the energy of these portals to reach high states of altered consciousness and procreate with the intention of bringing forth the star seeds.

The stone structure of today is a reminder of the significance of what took place on this sacred ground and echoes something otherworldly blocked by humans from their consciousness—that since the beginning of time, star beings have infiltrated our beloved Earth. However, if we look closely, that information has always been available to us. For example, indigenous cultures have long shared stories of visitations, creation, and migrations, and we have artwork from around the world depicting gods and goddesses of many cultures, all inspired by the visitation of other beings.

I believe the great stones of Stonehenge are a giant "X marks the spot" from an aerial point of view. To the knowledgeable observer, they outline where the portal is. Many people who travel to see Stonehenge report feeling the energy of the portal. Over the centuries, the energies present in the portals on Earth shift and change. Specifically, at Stonehenge, it has been blocked on the celestial side and no longer receives the Pleiadians who visited long ago.

The Ancient Ones told me that the energy at Stonehenge has moved deep into the earth and will remain there until the planet is once again cleansed through an ice age. The stones, however, are still charged with a high frequency direct from the cosmos and continue to transmit that frequency. Dr. Kieran O'Mahony, a professor at the University of Washington, Seattle, has said that, "every planet has a frequency that is unique and can be picked up through radio waves." This further defines the power of this planet and what many from our galaxy and beyond understood.

2

Skellig Michael

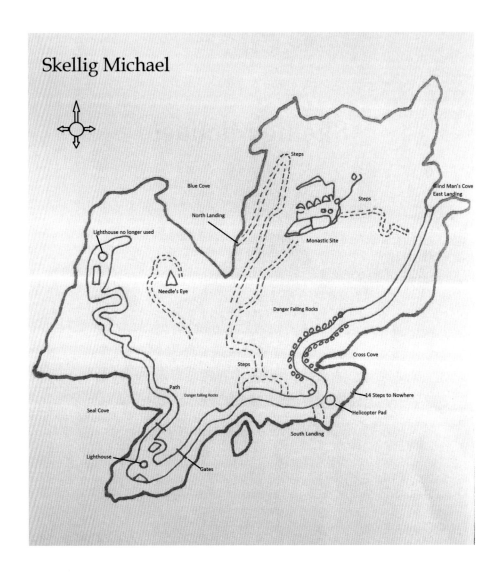

An incredible, impossible, mad place...
I tell you the thing does not belong to any world that you and I
have lived and worked in: it is part of our dream world.
—George Bernard Shaw, 1910

Of all the sacred places in the world, there is none more remote and mysterious than the towering, barren, and windswept sea crag known as Skellig Michael. Rising sharply out of the Atlantic, this inhospitable island is about 7.5 miles (12 kilometers) from the Irish mainland, on the south coast of County Kerry. The rock is also known as the Great Skellig, and it, along with its junior, Little Skellig, are located at the western end of what is the European landmass.

The name Skellig comes from the Gaelic word *Sceillic*, which means "steep rock," and this place fits its description perfectly, jutting over 700 feet (215 meters) above the ocean. An incredibly hazardous site, all visitors are warned of the very real risk of falling from its treacherous cliffs of shale sandstone. Yet today, they arrive in the hundreds to summit and reach the famed monastery at its peak—if, that is, they are not turned back by terrible weather conditions. Skellig Michael is a fascinating geological feature with cracks, faults, and caves riddling the base, where the rock meets the often-stormy water.

Remarkably, this inaccessible place was chosen by a small group of ascetic monks several centuries ago as the place to which they would withdraw from civilization to build a monastery and pursue a greater union with God.

Throughout its history, there has been something about Skellig Michael that penetrates the human psyche. The mists that regularly hang about its shoulders add to a sense of the spiritual. There is a belief that magic happens here, that secrets linger, and that ghosts keep watch over the gannets and puffins that now call this place home.

Any journey to Skellig Michael is long and dangerous. Even today, our modern boats can be tossed around by the turbulent waters, with the inclement weather adding to the uncertainty of a safe arrival. Who knows what the monks of the sixth century faced? Why were they so determined to settle there? Why did they build the beehive-shaped huts that still exist? Who are the ghosts said to roam the edges of the island? Did the monks use the many caves at the base of the rock for their survival? And what to make of the myths surrounding the ancient demi-gods, the Tuatha De Danann, and their influence upon the magical rock?

The Monastery

There are many questions about Skellig Michael, including the long-standing question of who exactly the first people to inhabitant the rock were. It is widely believed to have been the austere, self-denying Christian monks, known as the order of St. Augustine, who established a monastery at the site in the sixth century, but precise dating is difficult. The founder is claimed by the Catholic Church to be St. Fionan. His small group built the stone beehive huts in which they lived. However, it's a mystery how these monks survived, given the sparseness of vegetation, horrendous weather conditions, and inadequate shelter at this location.

Some historians believe the monks may not have been the rock's first inhabitants. In 2010, an archeologist by the name of Michael Gibbons discovered previously unknown steps and stairways, which lead off the three already existing stairways on the island. The stairways appear to predate those already known, and there is a suggestion that perhaps a fort-like structure may have existed on the site long before the monastery.

So, what evidence is there of the rock's history? The account of the death of a monk who lived on the island in the late eighth century is the first recorded evidence of Skellig Michael's existence. When the Vikings invaded Ireland, in AD 795, and stripped the country of its riches, Skellig Michael was sacked. *The Annals of Innisfallen, The Annals of Ulster,* and *The Annals of the Four Masters*—all early Irish manuscripts—have a little information about these raids, including the fact that in AD 825, the Abbot of Skellig was starved to death by the invaders.

We also know from these manuscripts that the Viking marauds on Ireland and Skellig continued. The invasions were always violent, murderous acts with a great loss of life. Despite recorded evidence of sackings continuing through the year AD 839, the monastery was eventually rebuilt around AD 860.

Interestingly, legend has it that in AD 993, the Viking leader, Olav Trygvasson, who was to later become king of Norway, was baptized on Skellig by one of the ascetic monks. In *The Annals of the Four Masters* there is a brief entry that the Blathmac of Skellig had died, and some believe it possible that this was the monk who performed the baptism. Later, in AD 1044, there is another recording of interest stating that Aodh of Skellig, another of the hermit monks, had died. Beyond these few entries in *The Annals of the Four Masters*, however, little else exists about the inhabitants of the island during this period.

In the 10th century, it is recorded that the monastery was dedicated to St. Michael. Then, for over 500 years or more, there seems to have been no other historical record of the site until 1756, when the book Ancient and Present State of the County of Kerry was written by Charles Smith. Records show that portolan charts used by the Spanish Armada map Skellig Rock. The island was the possession of the Order of St. Augustine until Queen Elizabeth I dissolved Ballinskelligs Abbey. The Butler family then inherited the island in 1578, and it continued to be a place of pilgrimage into the 18th century, even though the monasteries had been dissolved. A government body, the Commissioners of the Irish Lights, then purchased Skellig Michael in order to erect two lighthouses.

Of course, Skellig Michael is an Irish sacred place, so along with the hard evidence there are legends, myths, and wonderful Irish folklore associated with it. These stories of the Skelligs are ancient, and some involve the magic of the mythic Tuatha De Danann, an Irish group of demi-gods.

In the *Lebor Gabala Erenn*, or *Book of Invasions*, written in the 11th century, it is told that in 1400 BCE, Milesius, a leader of one of the prehistoric invasions of Ireland, lost two of his sons, when a magical storm invoked by the Tuatha Dé Danann caused a shipwreck. An upright stone slab, now vanished, which used to sit at one of the most treacherous parts of the island, was supposed to have commemorated Melesius's son, Donn.

Other legends, such as the Fenian tales, involve Daire Domhain who, in AD 200, was called the King of the World, and is said to have rested at Skellig Michael before beginning his attack on the nearby coastland at Ventry with Fionn MacCumhaill. Another legend tells how Duagh, king of Iarmumu in the fifth century, hid on Skellig while the king of Cashel was pursuing him.

Local folklore is rich with stories. One story possibly stemming from the visit of John Windele, in 1851, suggests that St. Michael's Church was built at a spot on the island used by Pagans as a temple for the ritual worship of dragons and serpents.

Skellig Michael is dedicated to the Archangel Michael, the protector and guardian of the Catholic Church, and the legend goes that St. Michael appeared with a host of angels on the island when St. Patrick banished the serpents and other evil creatures of Ireland into the ocean. The image it conjures is of all the snakes and creepy crawlers being tossed into the ocean by St. Patrick while Archangel Michael watches from the cliffs.

Another tale tells of a hollow in a stone by the entrance to the church that fills itself with enough wine every morning to satisfy the exact number of priests at morning mass. Yet another refers to a strange force on the island that prevents seabirds, which use the island as a sanctuary, from actually flying in and around the monastery. The birds walk, and only when they are outside the monastery enclosure are they able to fly again.

It's hard to imagine what it would have been like to arrive at Skellig in a *currach* (coracle) back in the sixth century. To begin with, it is nearly impossible to land a boat on Little Skellig, and equally challenging but doable to land on Skellig Michael. However, the monks created three different landing spots on the island, and from each one they built a stone stairway leading to the peak of the giant sea crag's northern summit and the monastic site.

Blind Man's Cove climbs a sheer face in the east, and was recently restored. Blue Cove is a gentler climb up the northern route to the monastery. The incredible stairway left by the monks is quite a feat. There are only about 20 days of the year when Blue Cove can be accessed because of the horrendous weather and ocean conditions. Of course, it is possible that the climate conditions several hundred years ago were milder and the monks' profound knowledge of wind and tides guided them to find the best place to put their hide-skin boats.

The third southern landing at Cross Cove is a strange one. To begin with, there are fourteen steps carved into the rock that are unusable and go nowhere. The other question at this landing point is how the monks kept their hide-covered boats safely out of the reach of the turbulent waters, which would have destroyed them if they had docked them there. The only explanation is that they lifted the boats from the water by hand or built a derrick to lift the boats from the water.

Of course, almost a thousand years ago, the geology of the sea crag could have been different. We know that land movement throughout Ireland has been quite significant, so it could be that the water level was lower, and perhaps a shelf of rock exists where the monks stored the boats. From the landing, there are 618 steps, which climb over 600 feet (183 meters) to the monastery site. They are uneven and extremely slippery when wet.

Today's visitors arrive at Blind Man's Cove and access these steps by walking to a junction above Cross Cove. Once all the steps are mastered, visitors arrive at the remains of the monastery, which is on a long, narrow terrace enclosed by a dry stonewall on the northern peak of the crag and sheltered from the prevailing winds. To find the six beehive huts, visitors go through a small tunnel in the retaining wall that leads to the main monastic area, the oratory, and the ruins of the medieval site of St. Michael's Church. There are also a number of other platforms containing crosses, as well as a cemetery with 22 grave slabs.

The six corbelled, beehive-shaped huts are where the monks lived. There was also an elaborately designed system to carefully collect and purify water in cisterns. Historians believe that no more than twelve monks and an abbot lived on the island at any one time. Just how they survived is hard to imagine, given that there was no fresh water supply and that the vegetation on Skellig is sparse and the currachs were not big enough to ferry large amounts of supplies to the island. The small garden site probably provided corn grown by the monks, who must have faced starvation on more than one occasion. In the summer, the monks ate seabirds, eggs, and fish.

The beehive huts were created from stones without using any mortar and are rectangular in their floor plan; they progressively take on a circular shape as the corbelling moves upward. The internal walls are straight to the height of 5 feet (1.5 meters) before the dome shape begins. Stone pegs protrude from the wall around 8 feet (2.4 meters) up; they were used to support a wooden upstairs floor. Windows high in the dome-shaped hut let in light at the second level.

All in all, the habitat and oratories are quite the architectural feat, considering the amount of labor they must have required. What's more surprising still is that the monks were able to construct a tunnel under the mountain, although no one has been able to confirm the location of the tunnel entrance, or even that it exists at all. We know about it primarily because legends tell of a subterranean tunnel leading away from the monastery.

The only other structure in the monastic enclosure is St. Michael's Church, now a total ruin. Interestingly, the stones used to build it were supposedly imported from Reenadrolaun Point on Valentia Island, an amazing achievement, seemingly nigh on impossible, given the ocean's stormy waters and tiny labor force available.

One of the uses for Skellig Rock in the Middle Ages was as a penitential station, and we know that one man was sent there for murdering his son. Centuries on, pilgrims arrived at Skellig Michael to climb the steps and follow the Stations of the Cross. They would then kiss the standing stone, which stood 712 feet (217 meters) high, above the sea at the southern pinnacle of the island and, as mentioned earlier, disappeared in 1977.

Giant Skellig was also the site, not surprisingly, of many fatal shipwrecks, including the sinking of the ship the *Lady Nelson* in 1839, which was carrying fruit and wine for the Lady Chatterton and bound for Oporto via London. The ship was smashed against the rock, and all but three people on board were lost.

Two lighthouses were built on the island about a decade before this shipwreck, and unfortunately, numerous people died in the building and servicing of them. One fell over the cliff while cutting grass for his cow, and tragically, several lighthouse keepers' children, who were growing up on Skellig, also died from falling off the cliffs. Hugh Redmond of Wexford, the first lighthouse keeper, lost both of his sons and his nephew over the cliffs.

Adding to the mystery of the secret tunnel on the island is the story of a surprise visit to the lighthouse made by the government commissioners in 1870. The lighthouse keeper, Thomas McKenna of Crookhaven, was discovered absent from his duties and duly dismissed. He was apparently busy exploring the underground tunnel in the monastery site and got stuck. A colleague brought him to safety, and the commissioners ordered that the tunnel be closed. Many speculate that this was the legendary tunnel of Skellig Michael, although no one has ever proven its existence.

A storm in 1951, considered to be one of the worst ever recorded on the island, caused damage to the lighthouse when a wave 174 feet (53 meters) high broke the glass lantern and flooded the light. The storm also claimed the road, boat landing, and cargo derrick.

Today, the lighthouse is automatically run, after the old one was torn down. Unfortunately, 146 years' worth of records and logbooks were lost when the old lighthouse was demolished and so, too, was much valuable research for today's understanding of Skellig Michael. The modern lighthouse is equipped with everything a mariner would hope for—a bright light, a sound foghorn, and automatic operation that does not need to be attended. The lighthouse is locked and the once warm kettle of strong tea and 160 years of boatmen visiting friends on the island is no more. Only the ghosts remain.

Spirit Traveling
to Skellig Michael

It is hard to describe the appalling weather my spirit guides and I experienced as we arrived at Skellig Michael during my spirit travel to the site. A gale blew so strongly that the cold rain slammed into our faces like sharp needles, and we could barely find a secure footing at the pinnacle of the rock. I was soaked to the skin, and we hurried toward the beehive huts, with the hope of taking cover from the storm as soon as we could.

As we rushed along the trail, leaning into the treacherous cliff side and looking down at the swirling waters, I was terrified that one wrongly placed foot would have me tumbling to my death. We stood for a second near the entrance to the huts, and as we did so a procession of monks moved swiftly yet silently before us. They were headed to the large oratory. The priest at the end of the line turned and looked at me. It was so difficult to make out his features in the near freezing downpour, but he looked sullen and drawn.

On instinct, I followed him into the largest beehive. Once we were inside, the noise of the wind and the rain abated a little, and I asked what the soaked priest and his fellow monks were doing. Before answering, he wiped the rain from his face on the sleeve of his cassock. "We keep the place going with daily prayers and rituals for the sun and the earth," he said. "We are more like Pagans than we are the modern-day Christians."

Could this be St. Fionan, I wondered?

The priest looked at me and said, "Yes, I am Fionan. I am of the first group of monks to arrive on Skellig Michael. We came to the island, searching for seclusion. We wanted to escape the world and practice what we felt were the true teachings of Christ."

I asked the priest what year he had arrived on Skellig.

"AD 489," he replied. "We are Irishmen. Our practice was peaceful, and we wanted to live free of judgment."

St. Fionan explained that he and his monks had built the huts and oratories, their only way to stay warm and protected. "We learned from the nature around us; the bees were our greatest inspiration. The way in which the bees construct their hives was the template for our beehive-shaped home's construction, and we figured out how to preserve our foods using honey and wax. We knew Skellig has magic; many of us had heard the tales of the Tuatha De Danann."

The priest gently took my hand. "Let me show you," he said.

As we entered the large oratory, I could see the monks sitting on the ground. There was a strong smell of damp rising from the stone. The light was dim, and a fire burned at the far end, the smoke escaping from a small window. One at a time, the monks appeared to move, and I blinked trying to clear my focus. Suddenly, I realized what they were doing—they were levitating. One at a time, with eyes closed and in a deep state of meditation, they rose from the ground.

St. Fionan turned to me, with a twinkle in his eye. "It seems some of the island holds you down, while other parts let you go," he said. "Many have died here, and not because it was their time. This island has a deep magic that rises from the earth and fills the spaces it chooses. We built the huts in this spot because it is where the energy chose these quarters to be."

Now all the monks were levitating simultaneously over the crude rock floor. Fionan continued, "Sit with us and try it."

I smiled nervously and took my place on the cold hard rock near the monks. The ground beneath started to move. My body became weightless. I looked up to my guides, who were gazing back steadily. Closing my eyes, I went into meditation and started to rise off the floor, moving with the flow of the airwaves. There was a rhythm, a sensation like nothing I had experienced before.

St. Fionan sat alongside me, waiting until I gracefully returned to the floor. "The Danann knew this place," he said. "They came here long before us, for ceremonies with the moons."

Once more, St. Fionan asked me to follow him outside. This time, we headed back toward the beehive huts and stepped inside. The air immediately changed. It was thick and heavy, and the wind whistled through the cracks between the stones.

"We slept in these huts," Fionan said. "There were 12 of us, and we slept two to each hut. They represented the 12 months and the 12 symbols in the sky. We would sleep with our heads in opposition, one in the north, and the other in the south. We understood the earth was held together by magnetic poles, something we learned from living on this magnetically charged rock. We would gain knowledge of these directions by sleeping in this fashion. We believed that our sleep kept the earth in balance. We also built the beehive huts symbolizing the earth. We slept in her womb, and we were the magnetic poles inside."

I asked St. Fionan to show me the 14 steps at the base of the Criss Cross path that reportedly went nowhere. I wanted to know what the steps were for. Outside, the weather was calmer, but there was still a biting wind.

We walked from the monastic site to the south landing and headed up the cliff to the infamous 14 stairs to nowhere.

The priest looked embarrassed. "There used to be an outcropping of rock, like a small landing, that has since broken off and fallen into the sea," he said. "This was built as a protection for the monks who were often raided by the Vikings. In a raid, the enemy would be directed by surviving monks to the boats below us at Cross Cove, via the stairs. Once they had descended the 14 stairs, the monks would inform the enemy that they would need to find the footholds under the rock to get to the next set of stairs. Only there were no footholds or stairs, and the grip of the enemy on the rock would be lost trying to find the foothold. It was the only defense we had."

I smiled and told him I loved their creativity.

We left the cliffside and began to climb once more, this time headed to the Needle's Eye. I followed as Fionan and the monks took me to the pilgrimage site. I must admit it was an amazing experience to walk up that hill with the procession of these ancient monks.

At the top, where the stone slab once stood, was Archangel Michael, standing before us. A brilliant light illuminated his angelic form, which stood larger than life. I thanked him and acknowledged how much I appreciate his help daily. He told me he was very happy that I was visiting the island and hoped I would spend as much time as I needed to understand the mysteries of this "mountain."

I wondered why he had described what I knew as a giant sea crag to be a mountain. Of course, I knew that the geology of the area had changed quite a bit over the years, and that before the European landmass was flooded things looked very different. Here was Archangel Michael confirming what ancient geology had shown to be true—that Skellig was a mountain rising out of the European landmass. The coast of Ireland was 20 miles (32 kilometers) to the west and way down below. Michael blessed me and touched my forehead, and St. Fionan smiled saying, "You were meant to be here."

Together, we turned back toward the beehive huts and the small oratory. We stopped at a point where some of the earth had been dug over and moved long ago. It was now overgrown.

"This is where the tunnel opening can be found," he said. "When we were living on Skellig, we dug into the earth, day in and day out, creating a tunnel deep into the rock and soil. We carried the dirt and rock out by hand. We used this chamber to connect with the earth and her magic. Sure, we prayed and held our spiritual beliefs in high regard, but we never forgot the source of our home. This chamber held magnetic energy that was even more intense than the large oratory."

Almost instantly, the wind grew again in intensity, blowing my hair almost straight and to the north. The landscape was changing before my eyes, and the once-sealed opening to the tunnel opened, and my guides and I entered, following Fionan.

A damp musty smell immediately filled my senses, and as Fionan handed me a lantern, I could make out carefully carved stone stairs leading downward. After descending into the belly of the rock for a few minutes, we then rounded a bend and a large room opened up before us. It was circular, about 10 feet by 8 feet (3 meters by 2.4 meters), and reminded me of the ceremonial chambers built by many indigenous cultures. Fionan brought the small lamp into the chamber. I gasped at what I saw. Skeletal remains of six men with books and crude candle bowls were strewn about. Shocked, I asked the priest what had happened.

"This was a terrible accident. The tunnel caved in, suffocating them as they slept. We never moved their bodies, because this happened long after the first group of monks lived here. We might have built this tunnel and chamber, but 100 years later, the tunnel wall was eroding and needed repair."

I began to feel uncomfortable. I could sense the energy of the earth trapped in this chamber and feared it would trap us there, too. I asked urgently to return to the surface. As we climbed out, I welcomed the wind and the rain against my face once more and heaved a deep breath as the fresh air hit my lungs.

We headed back to the monastic enclosure, with Fionan walking next to me. "We wanted the knowledge of the Tuatha De Danann. We incorporated their ceremonies into our daily practice. We had learned our Christian faith but still honored the Goddess and went into the womb (underground chamber) to give thanks. Our brotherhood was a strong bond that kept us alive."

Now we stood near St. Michael's Church. Fionan talked about how they survived by gathering eggs from the seabirds and growing corn, which they stored in the beehive huts. "We knew this land was part of an ancient history, and we wanted to know..." His voice trailed off into the distance, his attention drawn to the figure standing before us. The wind had stopped howling, and now the air was eerily still.

Danu of the Tuatha De Danann was in our presence. First, she turned to the priest and in Gaelic thanked him for showing me around Skellig Michael. Danu was a commanding presence, almost fierce. She waved us to follow her toward the large oratory. The rain had now stopped. Her blue eyes shone bright from her large frame, her blonde hair cascading down her back and shoulders.

"I am Danu of the Tuatha De Danann," she announced. "My people would sail to this island and hold ceremonies here for 21 days. We would start at the new moon and break our fast at the full moon, resuming our ceremony until the next new moon, after which we would leave the island as night fell. We used the magnetic energy of Skellig to recharge ourselves."

She looked out toward the ocean. "The energy of Skellig Rock, the wind, and the ocean will always charge you," she said.

She took my hand and led me to the edge of the cliff near the huts. Danu pointed to the ocean beneath us. "This ocean was much lower when the first monks lived here," she said with authority. "The shore of Ireland was farther. When the Tuatha De Danann arrived, it was centuries before the monks, and there was only land between the west coast of Ireland and Skellig Rock."

She flashed her blue eyes. Suddenly, there was land between Skellig and Ireland, just as there had been thousands and thousands of years ago. "This island was a great mountain in the time of Lumeria."

I looked out to the giant landmass before us. Where once there was ocean, now there was a vast expanse of land. I was astonished.

Danu smiled and said: "This was Lumeria back in 14,000 BCE. The people of Lumeria recognized Skellig as a sacred mountain. They were a highly developed civilization and understood the ways of the earth, technology, and alchemy. They flourished here. The landmass that was Lumeria fell into the ocean, but over time, the energies of the mountain remained, and the monks, knowing the ancient stories of Skellig, inevitably found their way to it."

Danu pointed over to the beehive huts. "The monks who came here long after us understood the power of this place," she said. "They would experience high states of nirvana in meditation."

Then, as her eyes seemed to cloud over with emotion, she continued: "When Lumeria broke apart, the landmass sank and the ocean rose to replace it. The coast of Ireland has few remaining remnants of Lumeria because the entire land mass has shifted much farther north."

Danu paused. She was more emotional now. "I felt it was a blessing to be here during the time before the great evil came," she said.

I couldn't take my eyes off her and instinctively moved closer. "A great evil was brought here by the followers of St. Patrick," she continued. "If people practiced the old ways, they were charged with death. They were murdered for believing in the sacred union between Heaven and Earth. We were forced to go underground."

Filled with grief, she looked downcast and about to cry. Instead, a smile grew across her face, and she said, "We will always be here. We will never leave this place. Only fools think we are gone from here."

With that, she grabbed my hand and we were airborne. Then in an instant we were standing on the landing of the lower lighthouse. My guides hurried behind us. The wind had picked back up, blowing my hair and cloak to the northeast.

"Do you want to know how they tethered their boats?" asked Danu.

Instantly, the ocean started to recede and rush down into the earth, returning the landscape to the way it once was during the sixth century. The island seemed to grow taller as Danu pointed to a ledge now visible, covered in barnacles. Once again, we floated effortlessly through the air to the now exposed ledge, and she pointed to an opening tucked under the rock at the back of the landing. It was big enough to slide a boat through.

We crouched and went through the opening. An enormous cavern opened in front of us, with several small boats propped up against the wall of the cave. In the center was an opening in the rock floor. You could see the ocean water crashing against the rocks.

"The monks would anchor their boats here, against the rocks. Sometimes the cavern would flood, but for the most part the boats would survive," described Danu.

Then, over the sound of the crashing waves and howling wind, I could hear voices—male voices crying for help, echoing eerily around the inside of the cavern. I crawled out onto the ledge. Two men were thrashing about in the violent water, yelling for help.

Danu shouted an explanation. "These men were shipwrecked long ago, and they are still trying to get rescued. They remain here for a reason—to teach others about the safety of sailing and how treacherous these waters can be. They have purpose. Do not fear, Sonja Grace. They, like the other ghosts on this island, have a reason for being here."

My normal impulse is to help souls to the light, and I felt so uncomfortable watching these men in such obvious distress. As I told Danu, she drew herself toward me, her eyes narrowing, and said, "Do not assume that is the path for everyone, for these souls truly serve humanity with their warnings."

I understood.

Then, shifting her attention away from the men, she pointed to the ledge we were standing on and said, "The monks had a pulley system to bring the boats to the landing. These monks were smart, and their knowledge of engineering far surpassed the time period in which they lived."

Danu took my hand. "Let's go to the upper lighthouse!" she said playfully.

Once again, we were airborne and landing gently on the grounds of the abandoned lighthouse. A man was visible, walking slowly around the lighthouse tower with a small girl, around five years old, who ran squealing with delight toward her mother calling from the tower.

"These people live here," said Danu. "They will never leave. They feel it is their duty to care for the island. Some people living on Skellig Michael became a little crazy because they couldn't handle the energy of the land. The monks were the only ones who knew how to manage this intense energy."

She turned to face the sea, and the light from the moon glimmered through her hair. Danu looked off in the distance.

"My people, the Danann, were guided to be here on Skellig. The land tells us many things, and our people understood the need to be respectful of this island. Too long here, and the energy could take over. Some have even died from this. Many who have died on Skellig still remain today as ghosts, their souls forever bound to understanding the energy of the island. The monks had great respect for this understanding. They built the underground chamber so they could tap into the womb of the earth and be reborn."

Danu suddenly looked intently at me. "It's time to go," she said. Startled by her urgency I asked why.

"There are so many ghosts here, and they all want to talk to you. You too are in danger of never leaving this place."

I looked at my guides, and we prepared to leave.

I thanked Danu, and as she embraced me she whispered in my ear, "I will see you again."

3

Tiwanaku – The Gate of the Sun

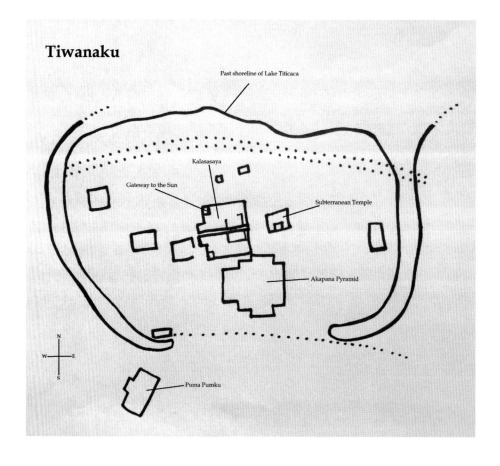

Tiwanaku

When the earth is sick, the animals will begin to disappear;
when that happens, the Warriors of the Rainbow
will come to save them.
—Chief Seattle

While Europe boasts the magnificent monoliths of Stonehenge in England, Carnac in France, and Gobekli Tepe in Turkey, continental America is also littered with mysterious megaliths. South America's Tiwanaku is perhaps the oldest and most enigmatic.

The Spanish conquistador and chronicler Pedro Cieza de Leon was one of the first people to write about it, when he stumbled upon the remains of the city in 1549. It is believed that no significant looting of the stones had occurred when he arrived, so his view of Tiwanaku and its other archeological wonders were in pristine condition, as if the explorer had stepped inside a time capsule.

Almost from the beginning of its discovery by the modern world, mystery has surrounded the site:

"I asked the natives whether these edifices were built in the
time of the Inca," wrote Cieza de Leon. "They laughed at the
question, affirming that they were made long before the Inca
and... that they had heard from their forbears that everything to
be seen there appeared suddenly and in the course of a night!"
—Brian Foerster,
The Enigma of Tiwanaku and Puma Punku: A Visitor's Guide

Tiwanaku or Tiahuanaco is a massive site, covering an area of about two square miles (5 square kilometers) across on the Altiplano plains in Bolivia near Lake Titicaca. At a dizzying 12,600 feet (3,840 meters) above sea level, where the air is thin, the site is the highest city in the ancient world. It is also believed to be one of the most ancient, with various accepted studies putting it at around 2,100 years old.

Noted Bolivian engineer and archeologist Arthur Posnansky claimed that Tiwanaku was created in 15000 BCE, according to archeoastronomical techniques. His findings were supported by German astronomers Rolf Muller, Hanns Lundendorff, Freiderich Becker, and Arnold Kohlshutter in the 1930s, but they were later disputed, as his research lacked any physical evidence.

Tiwanaku contains a number of fascinating archeological elements, from decorated monoliths, perfectly set stones, and remarkable stone masonry to sculptures, temples, pyramids, and even piles of rubble spread throughout the area. Most notable are Akapana Pyramid, Kalasasaya Temple, the statue El Fraile (the priest), Puerta del Sol (Gateway of the Sun), Puerta de la Luna (Gateway of the Moon), the Semi-subterranean Temple, Putuni, Kantatayita, and Puma Punku (Gateway of the Puma).

Akapana Pyramid is no longer as visually captivating as it likely would have been at the height of Tiwanaku's powers or when Cieza de Leon found it. Unfortunately, the pyramid fell victim to looters over the years—from the Spanish invaders looking for gold to local people using the original stone to build homes and churches. What is left is a rough square with a flat sunken oval area of about 172 square feet (16 square meters), built over an existing geological formation, probably an artificial hill.

Kalasasaya Temple is a giant red-sandstone-and-andesite platform, about 1400 feet by 1300 feet (427 meters by 396 meters), precisely fitted to a 32-foot-high (10-meter-high) platform. It is likely that this open space was used for ceremonies. There are clearly two types of walls, built using two methods: one with irregular blocks and the others with straight-edged blocks. Many of the blocks have grooves cut into them, which were probably used, along with ropes, to transport and position the stone blocks into place.

The precision of the blocks is just one of many indicators of a sophisticated use of measurements, transportation, and design, similar to that found in the Great Pyramids in Egypt. Monolithic uprights stand on either side of the entrance to the temple, which is accessed by massive steps. A restored portico leads to an interior courtyard and to the ruins of what are believed to be the priest's living quarters.

Also found at this temple site is the statue *El Fraile* (The Priest). The large figure looks like it is weeping and holds a beaker in one hand and a staff in the other. The figure is also covered in 30 small representations of animals and mythical creatures.

The impressive Puerta del Sol (Gateway of the Sun) is perhaps the most famous monolith identified with Tiwanaku and is also found at the temple site of Kalasasaya. Decorated with carvings, Puerta del Sol is believed to be associated with the worship of a sun god or some kind of calendar. It is made from one massive block of andesite, which weighs about 44 tons. Puerta de la Luna (Gateway of the Moon) is also found at this temple site but on the western end. It is decorated with animal carvings.

The Semi-subterranean Temple, a sunken structure made of red sandstone, is to the east of the larger Kalasasaya. The walls are decorated with tenon heads (massive stone carvings of fanged jaguar heads) and sculptures of human faces. Some archeological experts think that it may represent the underworld.

The large rectangular area west of the Kalasasaya Temple is still being excavated. It is called Putuni (Palace of the Sarcophagus). Kantatayita, a giant pile of geometrical blocks, was once some sort of a structure but is now rubble, and archeologists are trying to piece it together. Finally, Puma Punku (Gateway of the Puma) is another temple site containing giant megaliths, some of which weigh over 400 tons.

Construction and Builders

Attempts to understand Tiwanaku, how it was constructed, and by whom must first overcome one major hurdle: over the centuries since its discovery, the site has been subjected to numerous and haphazard archeological excavations and also has been looted repeatedly.

Archeologists believe that small peasant communities initially inhabited Tiwanaku, perhaps as long as 3500 years ago, and that somewhere between AD 300 and AD 1000, ancient South Americans added the megaliths and sculptures. Unfortunately, there has been no way to prove this time sequence so far, because the exact identity of the builders is unknown. Unlike at other sites around the world, the people who constructed Tiwanaku left behind little that ties them to a particular group or culture, and they appear to have had no form of writing system. Furthermore, local folklore is filled with stories about the site, none of which give any real clues to the actual builders.

Despite not knowing who created the structures, archeologists believe that Tiwanaku eventually rose to become the center of political, cultural, and religious power in the Andean region, with many people making pilgrimage to the sacred site to worship and praise the gods. Tiwanaku and its builders are likely a precursor to the Inca Empire.

The construction and layout of the site has several notable and puzzling features that have fascinated archeologists and historians for years. For example, the terrace walls at Akapana are constructed without mortar and consist of stones laid so tightly and with such incredible precision that a playing card cannot be inserted between the joints. This fact alone has led experts to debate what seem to be the advanced capabilities of the builders.

As with Stonehenge, questions arise as to how the large stone building blocks, which were quarried six miles (10 kilometers) from the site, and the green andesite, which came from across Lake Titicaca, 50 miles (80 kilometers) away, were moved to Tiwanaku. In other places around the site, there is evidence of an ingenious method of holding the stones together using metal brackets. Clearly, whoever did the stonework here knew how to work with molten metal and how to move the stones, some of which weighed in at over 100 tons, into place. Excavation of the upper terrace at Akapana shows that it was likely covered with green gravel, possibly decoratively.

Other stones around the site have been cut internally with stone channels that appear to be drains. There is also clear evidence of a moat surrounding three sides of the city, and archeologists suggest that the city itself was originally at the edge of Lake Titicaca. It is likely that the lake and the primitive drainage system found around the site were used to irrigate crops, and that water was moved around the city via irrigation canals, aqueducts, and dikes.

One of the most compelling questions about Tiwanaku is why such an austere environment was chosen for this site. At high altitude, it is cold, often dry, and the air is thin. No doubt, there have been some climate changes since the first stones were laid there, but even so, the territory of the Andean plains did not naturally lend itself to growing arable crops.

One theory is that the people who built Tiwanaku came from distant regions, near the foothills, and converted the marshy land around the lake area to grow the crops. Once they had drained the fields, the remaining soil would have been rich and provided productive agricultural land. However, at such a high altitude, nighttime frosts would have destroyed any crops they were able to raise.

Surprisingly, their solution of raised fields, a sophisticated idea for such a primitive people, appears to have helped Tiwanaku become an economic power. The city and surrounding settlements are thought to have been at their most vibrant and populous somewhere between AD 500 and AD 1000 and probably reached around 10,000 people. Experts think that the Tiwanakuns became such a powerful force in the region because of their innovative farming techniques and the abundant crops they produced. Remnants of this field system are still apparent at the site. Some experts believe those who converted the marshes and raised field system also created the sacred sites around Tiwanaku to thank the gods.

Many areas of the Tiwanaku site still need to be excavated, catalogued, and mapped, and as this happens many surprises and further mysteries about the religious, political, cultural, and economic history are likely to be unearthed. For example, some excavation work at Akapana Pyramid revealed 21 human skeletons. Markings on the skeletons show deep cuts and compression evidence, which leads historians to believe that people were possibly hacked to death, either during a battle or as part of a sacrifice, before they were buried at the base of the temple.

Experts think that Tiwanaku was laid out on a grid system. The axis of the complex faces the equinox sunrise, and the gates are aligned to other special days on the calendar, such as the winter solstice. It is thought that the gates around the site are symbolic gateways to the heavens. Recent surveys using ground-penetrating radar have shown that other man-made structures may be located at the site, such as buildings, a drainage system, terraces, and pavements in and around the temple at Kalasasaya and the Gate of the Puma (Puma Punku).

What all these buildings and subterranean structures were and what they were for is still not fully understood. Some experts think that the whole structure was an astronomical observatory. Myths and folklore about the site suggest that the sun and the moon are the islands in Lake Titicaca where the first race of stone giants, such as those depicted by the monoliths, produced the human race. Mythologists believe that early people considered Tiwanaku and surrounding sites to be the center of the world, and that the monoliths and structures were placed in alignment with the sunrise. However, over the centuries the earth has shifted on its axis, meaning that any markings used to track the solstices and the equinoxes are hard to find.

Religion and Mythology

Sculptures, pottery, and textiles found in and around Tiwanaku reveal sacred imagery similar to that found in other Andean cultures. The Sun Gate for example features the Staff God, perhaps the most often seen image in Andean cultures. This image shows the deity with fangs, splayed and clawed feet, wearing a headdress and clothes with snakes in them, and holding a staff in each hand. It is thought to be a representation of Viracocha, a sun god.

Some believe that the large stone structures around Tiwanaku were intended to represent the first race of giants in pan-Andean mythology or former Tiwanaku rulers and priests. The gold pins and remnants of paint found in some of the sculptures suggest that the sculptures were once brightly decorated with colorful paints or clothes. Other sculptures of puma-headed warriors holding a knife in one hand and a severed human head in the other, as well as the stone wall with heads sticking out of it, strongly suggest some kind of sacrifice to the pan-Andean decapitator god.

Further evidence of sacrifice can be found in and around Tiwanaku. Excavations have unearthed hallucinogenic cacti, drug paraphernalia, psychedelic entheogens, and mummified shamans with drugs and medicines. Hair samples from the mummies show evidence of psychoactive substances. They were even found in babies as young as a year. Other rituals are suggested by mass burial sites. One grave contained 40 males, all bearing signs of being cut to pieces. The fact that the remains are buried in an area of rain-deposited sediment suggests that they were sacrificed after a catastrophic climate event.

Decline and Fall of Tiwanaku

Furthering the mystery of Tiwanaku is the question of the fate of the people at this Pre-Columbian site and why it was abandoned so rapidly. Most prevalent among suggestions is the notion that the climate in the area changed dramatically around AD 950, with rainfall levels dropping significantly so that severe drought impacted food production and drinking water. Within about 50 years of the drought's onset, the area was completely abandoned. Significantly, this corresponds to the disappearance of other Andean cultures. However, the memory of Tiwanaku and the power wielded there lived on in the folklore and mythology of the people.

Spirit Traveling
to Tiwanaku

It was late in the evening. My guides announced it was time to leave. I took their hands, and in moments we were traveling through space and time. Soon we were high over the Andes, and Tiwanaku emerged from the darkness as if lit from beneath the earth.

We came to rest in front of the Gateway of the Sun. I adjusted my eyes to the dim light. My guides were staring into the distance. A glowing light approached. A flush of energy coursed urgently through my body, my face and fingers becoming hot. Instinctively, I reached for the steady hands of my guides and held on tight. All at once, an enormously tall man, approximately 12 feet (3.7 meters) high, emerged from the intense light and stood in its place.

This giant was fully illuminated from within, his skin pale and translucent. He approached and greeted us in a strange language, his voice coming through telepathically. Immediately, I understood. He told me he was Moowan, a traveler from Pleiades. He had come especially for our meeting and was happy to see us. The full moon lit the sky, sharing its light among the strange monoliths and constructs that are Tiwanaku. Moowan began to tell us his story.

"In the beginning, around 12,000 BCE, there was nothing here except for a small band of Indians living in the Andes. They came down from the mountains when they saw my people arrive as lights descending from the sky. We are demi-gods, and it was our task to help them create a thriving community and establish a temple in gratitude to the earth for helping our planet. We are from one of the many planets you call the cluster of stars Pleiades. Our particular planet is smaller than the one our brothers, known as The Ancient Ones, ventured from to help shape northern Europe."

Moowan beckoned me, and we began to walk together around the Kalasasaya, viewing the ruins. He talked about the massive statues, and how they depicted his people.

"This figure holding a beaker and a staff, he was our leader and a demi-god. The mythical creatures and animals represent his love for Earth, but he weeps for the human race. Diowa understood what would become of the people of Tiwanaku. He could see the destruction humans would bring to the earth. The receding water was a result of their behavior. Your modern scholars might believe the tears signified the rain. This is not so. During the time of Tiwanaku, our relationship to water was much different. We communicated with all water. This leader, Diowa, depicted in the statue *El Fraile*, was responsible for saving the Pleiadian planet. He brought back from Earth a crystal formation that holds light."

Suddenly, Moowan waved his hand revealing the place deep in the earth beneath Tiwanaku where the crystal was discovered. Moowan turned to look at me and said, "This site sits on many centuries of ruins."

Moowan urged me to follow him once again, and we crossed the Kalasasaya to the sunken courtyard known today as the Semi-subterranean Temple. He pointed to the tenon heads and faces in the walls, explaining who they were and why they were there.

"These are our people—the ones who helped build this place. We never showed our faces or our translucent skin; instead, we wore masks and ceremonial clothes to disguise ourselves. We did not want to reveal where we were from." He pointed to the stars. "We taught the people about the underworld. We showed them where we found the crystal and shared our knowledge of the earth's secrets."

We circled back around the Kalasasaya to the Gateway of the Sun, and Moowan continued his story.

"Long before these temples and statues were created this area was a portal traveled by the Pleiadians. Over the next 6,000 years, we taught ceremonies and rituals for fertility and rain, and we showed the people how to create unity through a clan-based system. The Gateway of the Sun is a marker for the portal covering the entire area known as Tiwanaku. It is our gift to the people. We gave them our technology and a way to join us when they were ready. When we arrived here, we came through the portal, emerging through a bright light. The indigenous Indians believed that light to be the sun. Consequently, the people believed we were from the sun. They built this gateway with its archeoastronomy and sun-god-like decoration to reflect that."

As I listened to Moowan's stories, I was aware of the parched ground beneath my feet. The smell was crisp, and the air thin at 13,000 feet (4,000 meters).

Now we were standing directly beneath the Puerta del Sol, or Gateway of the Sun. I looked up and noticed an eerie light surrounding the depiction of the sun atop the monolith.

Moowan continued: "The Gateway [of the Sun] was intended for the people to travel to our planet. We created a map that was kept at the base of a nearby mountain that only the early initiates were aware of. That information was passed down through the centuries and later used to escape a dark time in Tiwanaku. Many of them used the portal to leave and now live with us."

I looked up into the sky and could see the bright cluster of Pleiades. Moowan confirmed that this was the place to where the people of Tiwanaku disappeared.

"The entire complex of Tiwanaku was co-created by South American Indians and my people. We taught construction, metallurgy, and how to create stability within the giant stone slabs. Our technology for cutting and transporting stones is still not experienced in today's world."

Moowan pulled a thin translucent string from his robe and held it in the moonlight. He explained how this simple thread was used to achieve the exact measurements and precision of the cut stones. It was not made from any material I recognized.

We walked to the Akapana and stood near its outer edge. Moowan pointed to the ground, saying: "Underneath these ruins of Tiwanaku is the original city, built 12,000 years ago. Weather erosion and the ever-changing geology of the area have slowly destroyed what was originally here. However, the city was rebuilt, along with underground tunnels and chambers that run throughout the Tiwanaku complex. We were able to survive here for centuries in the high altitude due to our underground haven.

I asked Moowan when the pyramid was built.

"A large structure stood in the middle of Akapana, at the beginning of the city of Tiwanaku, and people gathered there for ceremonies and initiations. Three thousand years later, the people built this pyramid at the same time as pyramids were built in Egypt, Mexico, and China," Moowan explained.

He continued: "These pyramids represent a link between the demi-gods and a new phase for humanity. The pyramid was introduced for the purpose of connectivity between the Cosmos and Earth. It acted as a conductor of energy from the portal of Tiwanaku. Inside, the people conducted rituals, as well as dances for fertility. Men wore masks similar to ours, and the women were selected for their clan affiliation, initiation precedency, and offered to the demi-gods. They were taken into the pyramid's underground chambers, the womb of the earth, and the co-creation of mankind began."

"It was the task of the Pleiadians to guide the people of Tiwanaku. We gave instructions for a clan-based system into which young people were initiated through our ceremonies. They were to evolve into the leaders of the community," Moowan explained.

"The women were initiated into this society to work with the spirit of the plants and were in charge of seeds for crops grown at this high altitude. Their responsibility was to take the seeds deep into the pyramid's underground labyrinth and through specific ceremony ensure the health of future crops. They would plant these seeds after the ceremonies were complete and pray over their plants. Despite the arid ground and thin air, the crops grew each year and the people flourished with an abundance of food. Eventually, Tiwanakuns not only developed a strong relationship to the plant world but also created a bond with the animal kingdom. They understood the medicine of the jaguar and created ceremonies of their own revering the jaguar priests."

We moved through the pyramid site of Akapana back toward Kalasasaya, and I looked up at Moowan. I asked him how many years did he and the other Pleiadians continue to visit Tiwanaku?

"Every spring equinox, we would return to hold religious ceremonies for seven days with the indigenous people, to keep them together and prevent them from indulging in fear-based practices, such as sacrifice and brutalizing rituals. Once the people became strong and independent, we stopped coming to Earth. That was 4,000 years ago. By then, they had fully integrated our ways and were half demi-god and half human. They grew crops that flourished. The unique water system built into Tiwanaku gave them the life source they had worshipped for years."

Now we were in sight of Puma Punku and the mysterious land that stretched out all around Tiwanaku. I knew that archeologists had recently found the boiled bones of men, women, and children close by, inside circular chambers.

I hesitated to raise the subject of the human remains and the circular chambers, but Moowan explained: "The circular chambers found at Tiwanaku were the same as the kivas found at Chaco Canyon, left by the ancestors of modern Pueblo people. The circular chambers were the original ceremonial centers that were replaced by other temples over time. The kivas were a part of the original Tiwanaku."

Moowan moved away from me, staring up toward the stars. When he turned back to look at me, his face was taut and serious.

"The people grew restless," he began. "They were angry. Their water source was drying up, and their crops no longer grew healthy and tall. These bones are the bones of those sacrificed in rituals. They were misusing the sacred water and the medicines of the earth. These once peaceful people began to fall into darkness. They used the medicines to cloud their minds and broke the bond between the plant world and this. Eventually, they became barbaric in their ceremonies, dismembering their sacrifices to the demi-gods to appeal for our return."

Moowan's tone grew softer. "Unfortunately, the tightly knit community we built began to break down. The people began to divide, and a class system emerged that took precedence over the clan-based society we encouraged. The traditional people followed our teachings, but new leaders created their own power structure. It became fashionable to hold ceremonies for young initiates and attempt to outdo one another. Each ceremony reached for greater achievements, conjuring up deities through black magic rituals that were not related to us. These entities took hold of the people, corrupting their minds and hearts."

Now I saw nothing but sadness in the eyes of Moowan.

"The people's minds became polluted, and at the height of their civilization, they started to fall, overtaken with jealousy and hatred," he said. "As the water dried up, and more and more people were sacrificed in desperation, a small group who worked in secret found the map and used the portal to leave Tiwanaku. They believed that we did exist, and that we were there waiting for them. They understood we were there all along, carved into the stone, standing as statues watching over them."

As we made our way back to the Gateway of the Sun, he asked me if I would like to go through the portal with him. I said yes, and my guides held my hands as we traveled deep into space. My return to my office seemed centuries later, but the clock only noted that one hour had elapsed.

4

Hagar Qim

There is no greater agony than bearing an untold story inside you.
—Maya Angelou

The Mediterranean island of Malta and its sister island, Gozo, are part of an archipelago that lies in the center of the land-locked sea. It is speculated that these islands are the remnants of the lost continent of Atlantis. The larger island, Malta, is a fascinating place: dry, low, and geopolitically important, and it is home to the oldest and most mysterious megalithic monuments on Earth.

There are seven monuments in total, spread across Malta and Gozo and nothing like them has been found anywhere else in the world. Remarkably, they antedate Stonehenge and the Egyptian Pyramids. Maltese folklore suggests that the temples of Mnajdra, Taxien, Scorba, Ta Hagrat, and Hagar Qim, all found on Malta, were built by giants, and Malta itself is often called The Island of the Giants. Whatever the real story, they exist on one of the most historically compelling islands in the world.

Surrounding the Maltese Islands are Gibraltar, Alexandria, Sicily, and North Africa, and the history of these flat limestone islands has been determined by their proximity to these warring nations and key trading coastal cities and routes. Consequently, they have been conquered time and again by the Phoenicians, Romans, Arabs, Sicilians, French, and British. Neither island has a permanent river, but the coastal area contains many sheltered coves and inlets, which provided seafarers safe haven in storms and the perfect watery seclusion from which to launch ships.

Thanks to oceanographers and the new science of inundation mapping, we have learned that Malta was not always an island. Some 17,000 years ago, during the Last Glacial Maximum, the sea level around the world was approximately 395 feet (120 meters) lower than today, creating a land bridge that spanned from Italy to Sicily; Malta and the Maltese archipelago were the mountaintops to this extensive landmass. Paleolithic humans and animals walked from Europe to Malta 16,400 years ago! It is apparent that prehistoric Europe had total influence on the ancient culture that resided on Malta.

Once the ice caps began to melt, 14,600 years ago, the oceans rose, and the land bridge to Sicily disappeared. The peaks of Malta survived the rising waters. By 10,600 years ago, all that remained was the highest ground formed by the islands of Malta, Gozo, and Comino.

Historians believe that people from Sicily first inhabited the islands, arriving around 4500 BCE, after crossing the sea, to discover more about the landmasses they could see from their shores. Clearly they had the skills to build boats and were smart enough to take provisions with them in the form of animals and seeds. Evidence of the people and their way of life has been found in caves around the islands by archeologists.

They are believed to have begun construction on the megalithic sites around a thousand years later during what's called the Ggantija phase. Each one of the structures is considered a unique architectural masterpiece, remarkable for its design as well as for its artistic and technological achievements.

The most impressive and well preserved of all the Maltese monuments is Hagar Qim, strikingly evocative of all Malta's prehistoric sites and starkly located on the sea cliffs overlooking the islet of Filfla. The closest village to the site is Qrendi. Today, canopies cover the temple to protect it from the elements and preserve the stones, which archeologists marvel at for the finesse and precision with which they are joined. Only in the Valley Temple at Giza in Egypt is the same exacting stonework and craftsmanship to be found. Nearby is Mnajdra, a possible partner temple—so close, in fact, that some believe they are both part of a larger original complex. Both megalithic sites are also near the spectacular natural wonder known as the Blue Grotto.

Hagar Qim, which means "standing" or "worshipping stones," was excavated in 1839. It is unlikely that the site was ever fully buried because paintings exist from the 18th and early 19th centuries portraying the exposed larger stones. Archeologists believe that the temples were built during the phase in Maltese prehistory known as Tarxien. It is the last phase of the temple-building period lasting between 3000 BCE and 2500 BCE. Although there has been no radiocarbon dating or other archeological dating to substantiate the orthodox assumption of a Neolithic origin of Hagar Qim, it is presumed that the principal megalithic temples of Malta were constructed during this time. What's left of the site today consists of the ruins of three buildings, the main southern temple, the northern temple, and the primitive temple.

When compared to its predecessor at Ggantija, Hagar Qim's main temple has a slightly different and more irregular floor plan, especially in the main building, which looks like a cloverleaf from above. There is a view among historians that the cloverleaf shape represents the builders' view of nature and the circle of life, growth, and renewal. The layout of the main temple has six large circular rooms connected by one interior passage, and there is an open-air shrine set into the outer wall.

Hagar Qim is defined, though, by the impressive smooth-stoned façade at the entrance. Theories as to the reason for this temple's unforgettable gateway are many. The most popular theory is that those who built the temples during this period were competing with one another for size and aesthetics. The main temple surely created an impact that outshone other temples across Malta and Gozo.

The grand entrance to Hagar Qim's main temple faces the midday sun; while there is no definitive proof that any of the temples were built to reflect the movement of the sun and stars, it certainly looks to be the case, especially since we know that prehistoric communities worldwide observed and marked yearly periodic cycles with the movement of celestial bodies. Hagar Qim is particularly interesting from this point of view because of the unique way it is laid out in relation to the winter and summer solstices. This has been a source of many questions for archeologists and historians.

The site is oriented toward all directions; the main entrance has a south-easterly orientation, which lines up close to the winter solstice sunrise. Other orientations appear to have influenced the position of certain of the massive megaliths. The builders must have had some mathematical sophistication because they seem to have divided the angles between the solstices and the equinoxes when lining up the stones. They also divided the number of days between the solstices and the equinoxes by marking the sun's different positions. A fragment of pottery with a solar wheel was found at Hagar Qim.

So, who exactly were the people who built this site, and where did they get their knowledge? Were the equinoxes and solstices as important to the people of Malta as in other parts of the world, and if so, why?

Perhaps the most interesting example of the astrological influence is inside the Main Temple. In one apse, in particular (referred to as B on the map) is an inner enclosure made out of large, low-set stones slabs. At the back of that enclosure is a small elliptical hole. During the summer solstice, the sun's rays pass through the hole and light up one of the low slabs. The question is why? Was this part of some kind of ritual? And what kind of ritual? Were there ceremonial figures on this low slab when the temple was in use? Perhaps there was something special placed on this slab that was illuminated by the summer solstice sunlight.

Intriguingly the large room on the left has three "table altars" and a doorway to another chamber that is reached by three steps. What was this room used for? Was it used post or pre the ceremony or ritual?

Joseph Ellul, author of *The Hagar Qim Complex*, published as a letter to *The Malta Independent*, believed that thousands of years separate the three stages of construction at the temple.[8] The three stages theory was based on the different types of flooring found in each of the three separate temples at Hagar Qim. The Primitive Temple sits in the east, on the front side of the Main Temple, also known as the Southern Temple. The Five-Apse Temple, or Northern Temple, sits 98 feet (30 meters) to the north from the main temple.

These three sites were built at different times, and as well as the different flooring, there are other clues as to when they were built, including the progressively more complicated construction techniques exhibited by these ancient people. The first two layers of flooring are marked with fire, and the third layer is not marked at all. All three layers show different methods of polishing the stone in the main temple.

Primitive Temple

The Secondary Temple or Primitive Temple is found about 30 feet (9 meters) to the north of the main building; it is thought to be the first of the

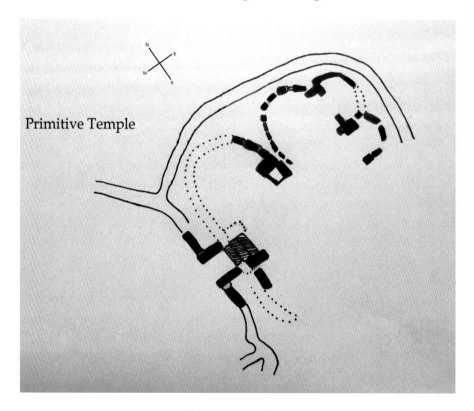

three buildings at Hagar Qim. It has suffered extreme damage from the elements. Many of the uprights have fallen while other stones show signs of disintegration. Originally, the temple consisted of two sets of enclosed areas parallel to each other. The first area is larger than the other smaller chamber that lies to the north. A polygonal niche was constructed in the front of the main passage, and to the left are two semicircular apses, one on each side.

Archeologists believe a thick wall once surrounded this temple and other temples on Malta. They have found stone balls of different sizes along the base of the wall. Scholars speculate the stone balls were used as rollers to transport the megaliths to the site, or that they contributed in some way to the foundation itself. Sadly, much of this temple is gone, and only some of the foundational stones remain.

The Northern Temple

The Northern Temple, or the Five-Apse Temple, is also mostly in shambles, with many of the stones of the outer wall destroyed from exposure. The

North Temple

entrance is in the northeast, with a rather imposing opening and a passageway about 20 feet (6 meters) in length. From the passageway there is an oval chamber with a semi-circular apse on each side. Through another doorway is another chamber with similar apses. The temple is small and described by some historians as shaped like a squatting god. Modern historians think the Northern Temple was used for the sacrifice of animals, because bones of oxen, pigs, and sheep were found during the excavation of this site.

The Main Temple

Hagar Qim's main structure, the Southern or Main Temple, contains the largest megaliths on the island. One, in particular, is absolutely massive, around 20 feet (6 meters) high and weighs 20 tons, and has rounded edges. The round edges are one of the elements that make Hagar Qim's architecture unique and puzzle archeologists. How did the builders move such large stones and fit them together so precisely?

The Bastion is an unusual feature of the Main Temple. It is a 65-foot-high

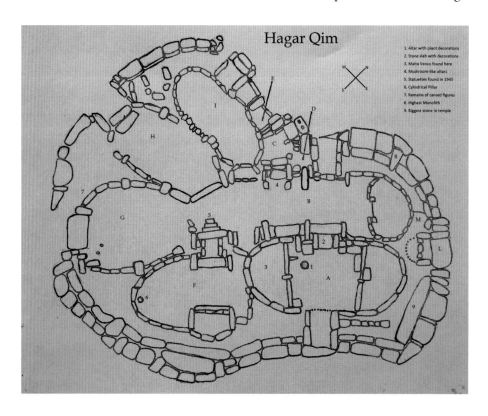

(20-meter-high) wall made from large stone blocks, which skirts the perimeter of the western side of the temple and curves in on itself as it reaches the outdoor shrine. There are differing theories for its purpose, with some archeologists believing it signifies the temple as a sacred space, while others believe it was constructed to keep out wild animals.

There are two other features inside the Main Temple that add to the mystery of Hagar Qim. The first is the number of altars inside—some very ornate, others quite simple, each one unique. Historians suggest that rituals and ceremonies occurred in these chambers and indicate that Hagar Qim was used almost solely for religious purposes.

Other clues to the past are found inside this ancient building. Its majestic opening, built using large, irregular slabs, hints at the grandeur of the place and the stature it once held in the community. A massive jumble of stones to the right of the forecourt is thought to be the remnants of chambers once used by those attending ceremonies at the temple, and a U shape that is deeply pierced through one of the paving stones suggests a fireplace. Although one of the ends is blocked up, there is evidence of the use of fire at one end.

Significant and puzzling discoveries have also been made over the years at the temple site. In the area marked A, about 10 feet (3 meters) past the entrance, is a smooth, paved central room with openings into further rooms. The central room has low stone altars, some discolored by fire and decorated with pit marks now almost completely faded away. In 1839, obese stone statuettes were found here, as well as a stone altar with deep carvings on all four sides, believed to represent a plant. They also found a stone slab decorated with spirals.

A passage formed by three large pillars leads to the area marked B, one of the most intriguing parts of the temple site. Clearly, there has been a remodel, but when is not exactly clear. Two deep apses once flanked the rectangular enclosure. Only one remains, in the east; the other was destroyed to create four independent chambers. Vaulted ceilings are detected, with the blocks and masonry built projecting inward in the apse to the right of area B.

It is in the remaining apse that we find an extraordinary feature that has captivated archeologists. The slab wall of the room is pierced with an oval hole about 16 inches from the ground. The hole opens to a small room (M), which is possibly the seat of an oracle. Archeologists call this hole the Oracle Hole, and believe that it was used for sound to pass back and forth from the main chamber into the recess; however, no definite use has been decided.

Numerous Oracle Rooms are found throughout Malta's megalithic temples. These oracle holes are also related to the astronomical alignment of the solstices and equinoxes. The architects certainly had the foresight and understanding to build these intricate sanctuaries and make them part of their spiritual practice.

Area B is the main hallway in the temple. In this passageway to the left is an entrance that leads to one of the holiest areas of the temple site. Within the elaborately constructed annex are well-smoothed slabs decorated with pit marks, now nearly invisible.

The small room (D), which appears insignificant on a one-dimensional drawing, is actually considered the holiest of holy in the temple, according to historians. A stone altar stands on each side of the doorway. Each altar bears an oblong top and a solid rectangular base. The raised edges are rounded and the foot of one of the altars is pierced by two elliptical holes, one above the other. The entrance to room D is well paved and flanked by slabs on end. A couple of conical pits connected at the apex are found at the threshold of the entrance, suggesting they were meant for rope hole. Similar rope holes have been found in Maltese megalithic temples and remain a remarkable feature of these so-called primitive people.

When Hagar Qim was first excavated, new areas were discovered that contained interesting features and objects. Strangely, those findings remained unclassified and reported for a long time. One of those areas was the so-called "Niche" and the rooms and areas surrounding it.

The Niche has an altar 30 feet (9 meters) above the ground supported by two pillars. To the right is another altar created from a single block of stone and deeply discolored by fire. In this enclosure, the passage becomes wider and a quadrangular area holds a cell at the end. A rectangular window-like opening is the entrance to a small cabin-like area. Based on findings in other Tarxien temples, archeologists think this room was most likely filled with bones of sacrificed animals and ritually broken pottery. It is thought that when burnt offerings were made, the horn or other body parts of the animal were cast into the cabin area as a memento of the sacrifice.

Another fascinating find was made in room G, which can be entered either through a gap in the wall of room F or an entrance on the southwest. Room G is oval shaped and the second of four inner rooms. Its floor, made of megalithic slabs, is lower than that of room F. Two figures with only lower legs and feet were discovered here, in the form of a decorative frieze on one of the slabs of the outer wall. These figures are similar to the sculptures that are characteristic of the Maltese Copper Age period.

Following the northeastern wall is another entrance that is paved with a substantial threshold. Standing at the site, viewers can see high slabs that have an imposing presence, followed by a stately group of megalithic stones. A niche flanked by two pillars is built into the recess of the wall (L). There are so many nooks and crannies in this temple, one could get turned around easily, but a conical pillar that is broken off at the top stands in this niche, and a pitted slab is placed in front of it on its smaller base, thus identifying this particular site. A deep recess or cabin is to the right of the niche formed between two slabs. The wall is pierced at the back by a large oval hole—the same type of oval hole found in the apse in B.

The question once again arises as to what these holes were used for? On the website *Places of Peace and Power: Temples of Neolithic Malta*, Graham Hancock also notes the astronomical alignment of this temple:[9]

> *Hagar Qim offers several alignments of the summer solstice. One, at dawn, is on the northeast side of the structure, where the sun's rays, passing through the so-called oracle hole, project the image of a disk, roughly the same size as the perceived disk of the moon, on to a stone slab on the gateway of the apse within. As the minutes pass the disk becomes a crescent, then elongates into an ellipse, then elongates still further and finally sinks out of sight as though into the ground. A second alignment occurs at sunset, on the northwest side of the temple, when the sun falls into a V-shaped notch on a distant ridge in line with a foresight on the temple perimeter.*

Chamber M was well concealed from view and speculated to be an oracular room. Double rope holes are found sunken into the base of two stones buried here. This room evokes a strange and spectacular feeling, one that leads to many questions. Were these rooms used for a special ceremony, and if so, who governed the activities at the temples? What was the purpose of the ceremonies at the temple sites and how did the construction and ceremonial purposes coincide?

In his article, *Mission Malta: Exploring the Sound and Energy Properties of Ancient Architecture*, on the website of Graham Hancock[10], Greg Kreisberg proposes one theory. He believes that the temple has a strong connection to sound and the use of sound as a possible form of communication with the gods, as well as use under the sea, as a weapon, connecting with the spirit world and altering consciousness.

Artifacts Found at Hagar Qim

Much of the academic fuss seems to revolve around the interpretation of certain humanoid figurines, most often identified as being, "anthropomorphic ceramics of the Neolithic."
—Linda Eneix, *Popular Archaeology*, February 2011

The most controversial aspect of the Temple of Hagar Qim is not the structures themselves but the statues and figurines found there. Stone and clay statuettes of obese figures were found at the site and are now displayed at the National Museum of Archaeology in Valletta. Three statuettes and several pieces of a much larger stone statue were found beneath a rectangular stone in 1949.

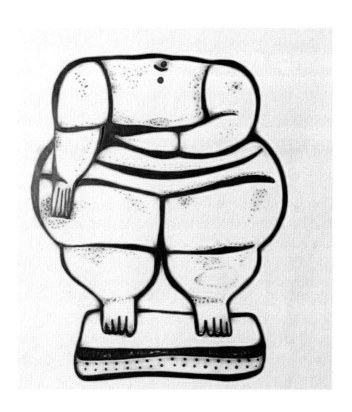

The most famous of them is called Venus of Hagar Qim. It was found next to room A and is possibly a symbol of a fertility cult, because it is abundant in proportion. What it does suggest, for sure, though, is that religion or ceremony and ritual were clearly the central focus of Hagar Qim and the ancient Maltese. Does this suggest a matriarchal society, one where priestesses populated the temple? The puzzling aspect of many of these statues is they appear to have little to no breasts, with the exception of the Venus of Hagar Qim.

Decorations found on the altars are of spirals and, unfortunately, their meaning has been difficult for scholars to decode since there was no actual writing at the time these temples were built. However, the finding of the artifacts and the decorative descriptions shows that art was central to Maltese life and a way of communicating and telling stories of everyday life on the island.

What frustrates most archeologists, historians, and scholars is the question of what happened to these fascinating people who built the intricately designed temples. Yet again, a population of ancient people with mathematical knowledge and engineering capabilities far beyond what we would have expected to see seem to have disappeared almost overnight. Like the Mayans, their fate remains a mystery, their deserted temples leaving only scant clues as to what made them leave. Was it war, plague, or something else that sent them fleeing?

Spirit Traveling
to Hagar Qim

For seven nights, I dreamed I was standing in a stone enclosure that had rooms and a central hallway. I heard babies crying and women chanting. On the eighth morning I woke up and, after reviewing the last seven nights, I asked my guides to take me to the place I saw so clearly in my dreams. My guides knew exactly where and what had been calling me while I slept. They told me that we would leave immediately, and we traveled through the realms to the most sacred site on earth: Hagar Qim.

It was still daylight on the island of Malta. I could smell the sea air and feel the sun's warmth as it rapidly moved higher in the western sky. I was standing in front of the first of three temples, and as I looked at it, I kept having visions of different time periods at the site. In one moment, women hurriedly entered the first temple; in another, seemingly much later in the evolution of the site, desperate people were running and screaming from the place. Clearly, I was receiving an unprecedented and massive download of the history of this sacred site.

Carefully, my guides approached and took me by the hand, leading me toward the entrance of what is the oldest temple on Earth. As we entered, I recognized this temple as the one known as the Primitive Temple, just outside what is considered the Main Temple. The sounds of women crying, chanting, singing, and screaming grew louder and echoed around me, increasing in volume with every step I took.

Suddenly, an enormous giant of a woman stood before me. She introduced herself as Pirme'aya.

"I am the goddess of this temple," she said. "It was built as a sacred place for worshipping the earth and holding ceremonies for fertility."

Pirme'aya bent down and, looking right into my face, said emphatically, "This temple was built for the earth." She said she had remained there alone, after Atlantis fell, to help the people of Malta.

I turned to look at the two rooms, which lay off the main chamber in which we stood. I asked Pirme'aya what they were used for.

She pointed to the first one and said, "All that is expressed as good took place in that room and in this one all that is bad." Then she pointed to the one on the right. "In all cycles of nature, we have birth and we have death. We can experience a range of emotions—from extreme joy to utter devastation in a moment, in a year, in a lifetime. I instructed the people to express these two sides through their rituals and ceremonies."

As she spoke, I found myself smiling and thinking about what I teach people all over the world. It was fascinating to me that the concept of dualism was being addressed with mysticism as long ago as the building of this ancient site.

Pirme'aya explained: "The room to the far north was used for preparation for all of the ceremonies. The room to the south was used only for rituals concerning fertility rights. Over time, this temple site has been changed; rooms have been added to accommodate the growing population of the island. Hagar Qim was first constructed in the year 8000 BCE, when the people were traveling back to the island from the mainland of what is known today as Italy and the island of Sicily."

Then Pirme'aya revealed that the Maltese people were escaping tribal wars in their original homelands across the continent.

Pirme'aya and I walked to the next temple, known as the Northern Temple. We stood outside. The sun was still bright but by now much lower in the sky. As we walked, I asked her when she had arrived on Malta.

She stopped and looked me deep in the eyes. "I arrived during the time of Atlantis," she told me. "Malta is one small fragment left of that ancient land. This massive civilization existed on the continent called Africa, which expanded all the way to Europe and to the west, including Spain, the Canary Islands, and Morocco. This giant land mass broke apart when Atlantis fell and was submerged under sea traveling with the shifting plates to Antarctica. I came with others to help with all that was Atlantis. We, the Tula, come from a sector of the Orion constellation. We are like other demi-gods who have traveled to Earth to help shape humanity."

She went on: "This massive land mass was attached to Northern Africa. Atlantis fell due to immense flooding and earthquakes in 10000 BCE. The people started to migrate north and built shelters underground, where the land was much higher. They knew a great flood was coming. We advised the people where to go and warned them. Some listened, and some did not. Those who did went far inland, where the floods would not reach and built underground rooms in the land that is now known as Turkey. Many stayed underground for a long time. Even the Canary Islands, which were also a part of Atlantis, have cave dwellings in which the people lived while the land shifted and oceans grew.

"The people of Malta built underground chambers centuries later, in case there was another catastrophic event," she continued. "The stories of Atlantis were passed down and fear kept them alive. They faced turbulent times again when the weather changed in 5800 BCE."

Pirme'aya looked off in the distance. She paused a moment, then took a few steps forward and asked that we follow her into the temple.

A chill passed through me as we entered the Northern Temple; concerned, I looked at my guides, who also seemed alerted. There was a strong sense of death in the air. The rooms here were similar to the rooms of the first temple, echoing size and shape in construction but built in the year 5800 BCE, before the great storms.

Pirme'aya said: "This was a difficult time for the people. They held onto their fertility rights, but as the weather wiped out their crops they sacrificed animals to appease the gods. The apse, that held all that was bad and evil, grew bigger than the room that held what was good.

"During the use of this second temple, over the course of 200 years, there were turbulent times, and the priestesses of Hagar Qim grew desperate. Stories of sacrifice were passed down, and the people decided their luck would change if they built a new temple. They would pray to me and ask that the gods have pity on them.

"Life on the island became increasingly difficult, and my people, the Tula, who are demi-gods, came to visit me and help create balance once more for the villagers of Malta. On many occasions, they would walk amongst the Maltese as if one of them. The villagers knew of our ability to transform into human form and were always aware. The statues of men found on Malta are, in fact, men from the Tula tribe who were the only men allowed inside the temples. They would visit me twice a year and bless the people with their guidance and fertility."

She smiled and brushed her dark hair, which contained small twigs and leaves, from her shoulder. She was ornate with earth elements in her clothing and hair.

She led us to the Southern Temple, or Main Temple, and I watched her 15-foot-tall (4.5-meter-tall) frame glow in the light of the sun as it dipped beneath the horizon, setting the sky into a glorious glow of red light. It seemed fitting that we were entering this temple under such lighting.

I once again heard the babies crying and women chanting, as we walked through the opening of the thick megaliths that framed this sacred place. I asked Pirme'aya why I had been dreaming of this place and hearing babies crying and women chanting.

Suddenly, I saw a procession of pregnant women passing us. The high priestess walking with them bowed to Pirme'aya and said thank you in a language that seemed too old to even exist. Pirme'aya said, "It is time for you to learn what went on at the heart of the Universe."

I looked at her with wide eyes and repeated slowly, "the heart of the Universe?" She turned into a yellow-gold light that illuminated the entire temple. I could no longer see her body, only a brilliant light.

The High priestess motioned for us to follow her. As we walked down the corridor, I observed the temple was designed in a circle, with events and activity moving clockwise in each part of the temple reflecting different times of the seasonal calendar. We glanced into the first room, and near the fireplace I could see a woman laying with a man. I thought to myself, *Well, this is obviously the room used for procreation!* Pirme'aya looked at me and smiled. Next we walked past an apse with a woman giving birth. Chanting attendants were assisting the mother as she gave birth. I smiled as I recognized the crying baby from my dreams.

The following three apses all have entrances from outside the temple. One was for doctoring and healing, the next for all crops to be blessed, and the third for initiation rites and the blessing of newborn babies once they were delivered inside the temple. We looked in and could see the priestesses rubbing oils and herbs on the newborns and taking care of the resting mothers.

The central room led to two more apses. Between the apses stood a sacred stone. The High priestess spoke to us in a low whisper: "An ancient tradition with the Tula has been maintained over hundreds of years that one room holds all that is good and one room holds all that is bad; therefore, keeping the balance of the temple and the Universe."

My guides, their mouths closed, began to hum a deep pulsating sound that reverberated throughout the temple. I looked at them and realized I needed to step into these rooms. I went into the room the High priestess had described as "filled with the goodness of the Universe."

I felt strange, as if all the energy in my body was being sucked away; yet, I felt overwhelmingly good, as my energy was joining with the positive energy that consumed the room. I knew I could not stay here, no matter how good this felt to me. My understanding of how energies "play" in the Universe meant that I knew this was only one side of the duality, and I braced myself for what I knew I needed to do next.

The humming of my guides grew in intensity with almost a crescendo of beats as I stepped into the opposing apse. My stomach churned and my throat tightened as I crossed the threshold, to be met by an intensely evil energy that filled every available space in the room. Entities crawled the walls, and horrific images filled my mind. Once again I was in a vacuum, but this time it was negativity. Here there was no goodness, only darkness and pain.

I gasped for air and fled from the evil's magnetic pull. I stood by the sacred stone and swallowed the clean air, calming myself with every breath.

The High priestess said, "This is what happens when the world is not in balance. One side is experienced without knowledge of the opposite." She moved closer to me and said in a low voice, "There is no happiness in just the good, and there is no sorrow in just the bad, for both need one another to be whole."

As she spoke to me, I noticed that, of course, I was standing right next to the sacred stone, perfectly placed exactly between the two rooms, and I felt a state of balance once again. I could smell an odor that resembled incense as a group of priestesses walked by, heading for the Niche, which held the oracle hole.

Pirme'aya had reappeared and was back standing next to me. She said: "They are preparing for the solstice. When the sunlight pierces the oracle hole, it will bless the statuettes that are all lined up, watching the priestess prepare each ceremony. These statues are of all the ancient goddesses who assist from the Tula."

We stood and watched the high priestesses as they lit a fire in the fire pit and began to chant, with the sound of their voices creating a feeling of intoxication. Sound carried through the entire temple as if a surround sound speaker system was in place! I looked up and saw what appeared to be local women coming through the doorway of the temple. They were asking the priestesses to bless their pregnancy or newly born baby.

"The local women all come here to have their babies in this sacred space. Through the special blessing performed by the priestesses, the agriculture of their village will be strong," said Pirme'aya, pointing to the baskets of grain that were also to be blessed during the ceremonies.

The High priestess added, "The crops were as important as the birth of a child and were treated with the same reverence and respect."

Pirme'aya spoke next. "This temple flourished, as did the people and all who were blessed by the priestesses. The statuettes that were found at the site were of the women who gave birth to the children of the Tula. They represented the earth and her large body, and the reason there are no breasts on any of these statues is that breasts would have shown a more human nature, when in fact these children were children of the gods. These women who bore Tula offspring were revered and sculpted large to match the stones that the earth provided to house their goddess. They were large in the hips and legs, to show the strength of their commitment to bring forth life. It also showed their abundance of wealth, bearing healthy crops."

Pirme'aya led us through the door, and we stood in the night air under a canopy of stars. "There is the Universe inside this temple," she declared, as she pointed to the stars. Once again she was looking right through me. I felt her eyes like warm light penetrating my heart.

Pirme'aya said, "I am the daughter of the earth, and when I left Hagar Qim, around 2010 BCE, it was because the island was invaded. Men came in war parties and raped the priestesses and took the heads of the statuettes that lined the shelf where the solstice light blessed them each year. The invasions left many dead and the priestesses beheaded, along with the women of the village. The invaders feared their magic and destroyed much of what was created inside the temple. Heartbroken, I felt it was time to return to my home."

I could see the constellation of Orion twinkling overhead. I smiled at Pirme'aya and the High priestess and said, "How lovely to create the Universe inside a temple built from stone." For a moment, I could see the earth forming and rocks moving into mountainsides and land masses shifting.

My vision returned to the night sky. I thanked Pirme'aya for all that she had shared with us. My guides held her hands in appreciation, and we exchanged one last look that will stay with me for the rest of my life. Her eyes turned crystalline blue and lifted me up into the stars, where my guides then whisked me home.

5

St. Winefride's Well

That whosoever on that spot should thrice ask for a benefit from God in the name of St. Winefride would obtain the grace he asked if it was for the good of his soul.
~ St. Beuno, British saint, died AD 640

St. Winefride was a noblewoman born around AD 600 in the Welsh town of Holywell in the county of Flintshire in Britain. There are many versions of the spelling of her name. I am choosing to use the spelling the historical site itself uses in its publicity materials and documentation. Along with the various spellings of her name go the various versions of her life story. Historical manuscripts, legends, and folklore may vary regarding the exact details, but the one constant theme is that of a pure, gifted, and beautiful young woman utterly devoted to living a life dedicated to the divine.

Winefride was passionate about living a consecrated life. She was determined to remain unmarried, and under the guidance of her uncle St. Beuno, a renowned priest and missionary, she was preparing to enter the Church as a nun even as a teenager. Her beauty and goodness were widely recognized in Flintshire and in counties beyond. There are a number of interpretations of the next part of her story, however; it appears to boil down to unrequited love.

Prince Caradoc, a nobleman who reportedly lived in a nearby town, traveled to Holywell to meet the beautiful and talented Winefride to ask her for her hand in marriage. Legend has it that when he arrives at Winefride's home, he finds her alone. He is immediately struck by her grace and charms and becomes ardent in his desire to have her be his wife. He makes advances, pleads with her, and even threatens her. Winefride refuses him. She is terrified by his intensity and by the threat to her deeply held wish to live a life of devotion. As soon as she is able, she finds a moment to rush away towards the church of her uncle, St. Beuno, who is holding a mass.

She runs as fast as she can, but unfortunately, Prince Caradoc catches up with her on a slope leading down to the church. Filled with rage at her continued refusals to accept him, Prince Caradoc raises his sword in anger, and Winefride is decapitated. Her head is said to have rolled and rolled down the slope until it came to a stop nearby the church. According to legend, a spring of natural drinking water immediately emerged in the spot where her head came to rest.

Upon hearing the news of the death of his beloved niece, St. Beuno rushes to the spring and gathers up her head, taking it to her body. Once able to unite them, he performs the Holy Sacrifice, considered by Christians to be the most powerful spiritual aid given to man, and Winefride is miraculously resurrected. The only evidence of her decapitation that remains is a faint white circle around her neck. Winefride is restored to full and vibrant health. God, on the other hand, strikes down Caradoc, and the earth is said to have opened up and swallowed him.

Following these miraculous events, Winefride fulfills her desire to live a virtuous life of devotion. She becomes an abbess at a convent built on land owned by her father. The people believe her to be a mystic. Later, she seeks refuge in Gwytherin, with St. Elwy, where she is said to have lived the life of a saint on Earth until her second death, 22 years later. She was a real person whose legend became famous. This extraordinary Welsh woman was venerated as a saint from the moment of her death.

The well, created by the spring that emerged at the site where Winefride's head came to rest, became a site of healing and pilgrimage. St. Beuno is believed to have seated himself on a rock by the spring and made a promise to the people in the name of God, stating: "Whosoever on that spot should thrice ask for a benefit from God in the name of St. Winefride would obtain the grace he asked if it was for the good of his soul."

Consequently, for almost 1,400 years, people have traveled to Winefride's Well and bathed in the waters and prayed for miracles. Surviving records claim cures dating back to the 12th century. Pilgrims have arrived in the thousands to bathe in the waters of the well—so many, in fact, that a railway line that terminated in Holywell was added in the late 1800s. Families carried loved ones on their backs through the water, and hundreds of crutches were left behind by those cured by the waters of the well. So many miniature shrines were built attesting to the healing properties of St. Winefride's Well that the town of Holywell became known as the "Lourdes of Wales." The well is perhaps the oldest site of pilgrimage in all of the British Isles and mentioned in a famous medieval poem, "Sir Gawain and the Green Knight."

Today

Visitors and pilgrims to the well today will find a beautiful and architecturally unique building. Royal masons built the two-story shrine for Margaret Beaufort, the mother of King Henry VII. It is set in the hillside and is close to a well-traveled road. Visitors, though, are struck by the silence surrounding the building, which is richly embellished with images of animals and the royal insignia of Henry VII and Thomas Stanley (third husband to Margaret Beaufort).

The ancient monument is still used today, and the spring water rises from the original spring into a basin and is accessed by steps. The water flows into a swimming pool, where the sick can bathe and enjoy the waters.

While the tale of the chaste nun who is beheaded by a suitor, then brought back to life, could never have really happened, there is no doubt that this legend is based on something. But what exactly? In my spirit travels, I will reveal the beginnings of the spring at St. Winefride and the truth behind her, the creation of the well, and the power of the Church in AD 600, as I travel through the realms to the time of the real St. Winefride.

Spirit Traveling to St. Winefride's Well

As I looked out of my window, I noticed the stars were exceptionally bright. My guides came to me and held my hands as we spirit-traveled across the Milky Way.

We arrived in the cold dark mist that surrounded Saint Winefride's Well, the fog adding a cloak of silence. There was a faint white light that came from a centuries-old statue of the sainted nun, and we walked toward it. Behind her, I could make out the outline of the ancient church. Beneath its arches was a pool of water shimmering with an internal source of light.

My guides let go of my hands and dropped back a pace to stand behind me. I looked into the pool, and the light gave way to the faces of the people who had been healed at the well. Instinctively, I reached into the pool and the water moved and shifted, illuminated as if phosphorus were present. It felt cool and creamy, and I cupped my hand, gathering the sacred water. I placed it where my body needed to heal and drank a small amount. As the water entered my body, I felt immediately grounded and connected to the sacred site. I looked up and the Savrock were standing there.

The Savrock people are tall and dark skinned, with a wisdom in their eyes that goes beyond all time and space. My first encounter with the Savrock was in deep meditation. I traveled with my guides to the center of the Universe, where the Savrock stand as gatekeepers between this world and the next. They are charged with Earth's care and protection, having been here since the beginning. The Savrock gathered in a circle around me, and the architecture of St. Winefride's Well disappeared.

I found myself standing on bare ground, with only a small pool of water bubbling there. The ground became transparent, and I could see deep into the earth. The Savrock began to show me how they created an underground world, with tunnels leading to rich lakes of emerald-green waters. The Savrock knew how to find these healing waters and assist humans in receiving them. They explained that the well in Holywell was one of hundreds deriving from deep in the earth. Water is the conduit that marries us all together, the Savrock explained to me. The sacred water was brought to the surface in the form of springs.

Geologists know that after the last ice age, 12,000 years ago, the land around Great Britain and the climate warmed. Fresh water springs began to pop up throughout Britain over the course of the following centuries. As I stood with the Savrock, they show me centuries of people using these springs as both a water source and for healing. High priestesses, who were often the leaders of these early people, were also in charge of caring for the water and understood the healing properties of the wells. The pagan ceremony of Well Dressing, honoring the water, still goes on today throughout Britain.

The Ceremony

In 4000 BCE, the Druids created rituals from the teachings that were in place 4,000 years prior. Slowly, the venerated high priestesses' positions as caretakers of the sacred water and wells were taken over by men who were initiated to lead the ceremonies for the Druids. Both priests and priestesses honored the goddess and the earth, acknowledging the source of all sacred springs. The Savrock showed me the rituals performed before the Druids came along, which involved the people coming to this humble site at Holywell and dipping their hands into the water and cleansing their body from all illness.

I watched as a high priestess of 10,000 years ago called upon the goddess to heal a sickly child who could barely stand at the spring. The high priestess washed the child, using rosewater and mint essence mixed with the sacred water. Gathering up the child in her arms, she laid him on an animal skin and started to circle her hand over his body in a clockwise motion. As she did this, she appeared to be activating the energy of the water. Before my eyes, the goddess of the earth appeared and touched the child in the area of his heart. The illumination from the energy at the site was astounding.

The high priestess bent over the child, rubbing the water mixture into his temples, his forehead, his chest, and all areas of his body. The lifeless form started to move and opened his eyes. He sat up and drank the sacred water. Feeling invigorated, the child stood. The high priestess placed a necklace of herbs and flowers around his neck, and he ran toward his family. The Savrock explained that stories of these miraculous healings were passed down from century to century.

St. Winefride

All of a sudden, I saw an extremely beautiful and serene Welsh woman standing in front of me! As I stood up, I noticed that the landscape around me had completely changed, and the stone building structures that surrounded the well, which still stand today, were now in place.

St. Winefride greeted me, indicating she was happy to see me at the well and acknowledged that she knew of me. St. Winefride offered her delicate hand to me and began to speak in a quiet, unassuming voice.

"The earth has certain places that are designated for healing, and these waters are to be used for that purpose. Do not forget the earth. She has given so much, and it is our duty to care for her. The well and all that she provides to us is a blessing upon our souls."

The light seemed to play on her form, and her hair was illuminated as it flowed down her back. She moved with grace, and carefully took my hand and led me to a stone at the well's edge. Hesitantly, I asked her what we all long to know: the truth of the legendary story of St. Winefride. She smiled and told me a story I will never forget.

"In my 15th year, I met a young man in the village not far from this site, here in Holywell. We fell immediately in love. We were everything to each other and looked forward to the day we could be together as husband and wife. Unfortunately, I was raised in a pious family, and my parents forbade any contact with Pagans. So we were forced always to meet in secret. Unbeknown to me, my God-fearing parents had promised my uncle, the high-ranking priest, that I would be a devotee. My life was to belong to the Church, and I was forbidden to marry.

"One day, my love and I were uncovered, and my father was furious and would not speak to me. He held a private meeting with my uncle, the priest. My uncle promised my father to prevent the marriage and make an example of us. Pagans and Christians were never to be together, nor was I ever to be allowed to marry. I was to become a nun, and my parents would turn away every suitor.

"Heartbroken that my father had discovered my love for the pagan boy and would not approve our being together, I ran away to this very site.

"My uncle, in the meantime, hired Prince Caradoc to chase down my love. He hunted through every village until he came upon him and, with a swing of his sword beheaded him, murdering him right on the spot. Caradoc returned to the village with my lover's head, and the priest had it put on a spike.

The priest made the announcement in the village to let it be known that Pagans and good Christians were not allowed to marry.

"The Pagan boy's mother came to me, distraught and wretched from the news of her son's death. She kneeled down beside me and shared the horrific news. When I heard what had happened, I began to cry, my tears spilling out into the spring. At that moment, water began to bubble up, expanding the spring into a large well.

"I beat the ground with my fists and cried out against God, begging him to explain such an atrocity. What was my life to be? What was my purpose now? It was in that moment of spiritual crisis that my heart connected with the source of this healing water and was flooded with compassion and love. It took all of my strength and effort to get up off the ground and face my future. My life was often solitary because of the sorrow that I carried inside, but I embraced God's need for me to be in service. I missed my opportunity for love; however, I chose to be in service for a greater purpose."

I noticed her devotion to God had cleared a pathway for her to heal, and the loss of this love created an understanding and compassion that is present at the well.

Winefride and I kept talking for what seemed to be hours. As the morning light filtered over the well and the surrounding stone buildings, our meeting drew to a close. The last thing she shared with me was that I, Sonja, had work to do around the globe. All I knew was that, as a healer, I did not want to leave this place. St. Winefride bade me farewell, and the Savrock gathered around me and escorted me home.

6

Chichen Itza and the Temple of Kukulkan

Look up at the stars and not down at your feet.
Try to make sense of what you see,
and wonder about what makes this universe exist. Be curious.
—Stephen Hawking

For thousands of years, the Mayan civilization thrived throughout the Yucatan Peninsula in southeastern Mexico. Royal cities with ornate temples oversaw vast kingdoms with abundant agricultural resources and lived in relative peace trading with one another. The people mapped the heavens, mastered mathematics, and had a primitive writing system. This Mesoamerican civilization even developed a calendar system upon which our own is based. Then, sometime during the eighth and ninth centuries, this powerful and advanced culture suddenly declined, and experts have wrestled with the reason why. Was it drought, disease, migration, or invasion that brought an end to this great civilization?

Over a period of a thousand years, the Maya and Toltec peoples left their vision of the Universe carved deep into their stone structures. There can be no doubt that the temples of the Yucatan Peninsula are a feat of engineering genius, and they continue to fascinate historians, archeologists, and visitors alike. The construction of Chichen Itza combines sophisticated building techniques and stunning architectural design that make it one of the most important historical structures of the Mayan-Toltec civilization. It leaves all who go there lost in admiration and wonder.

Geologically, the whole Yucatan Peninsula is a vast plain of limestone, with no rivers or streams at the surface—not an immediately obvious place to build grand temples and establish thriving cities. However, the Mesoamerica people settled Chichen Itza close to two natural sinkholes known as *cenotes*, or *chenes*, which reveal that the water table was at the surface at Chichen Itza in AD 415–35. The name Chichen Itza means "at the edge of the well of the Itzaes."

Water is a vital resource for any community, but as is true of numerous other Mayan temple-cities, Chichen Itza is also influenced by sacred geography. That is, its leaders chose locations for their temples based on mythology, symbolic landmarks, the astrological position of various celestial objects in the night sky, and shamanic factors.

The striking *Cenote Sagrado* (Sacred Well), which is one of the most impressive landmarks in the immediate area, is almost 200 feet (60 meters) across and surrounded by steep cliffs on either side, with the water about 90 feet (27 meters) below. Its easy to imagine how the sun playing on the water, the vines hanging from its steep cliffs, and the vastness of the place dazzled those who first stumbled across it. The Mesoamerican peoples revered this well. Archeologists have found evidence of this worship in the form of objects such as gold, jade, wood, cloth, and the skeletons of children and men at the bottom of the water, which suggests that the Cenote Sagrado was considered a place of pilgrimage, and possibly a site of sacrifices, particularly during a drought.

Chichen Itza was a city of impressive structures. In the northwest was the Great Ball Court; the Tzompantli (Rack), known as the Wall of Skulls; the Jaguar Temple; and the House of Eagles. The northeast was home to the Temple of the Warriors, the Group of the Thousand Columns, and the Market. In the southwest of Chichen Itza was the Tomb of the High Priest and the Caracol, a single, circular observatory with a spiral staircase, which lies farther south. El Castillo (the Castle), otherwise known as the Temple of Kukulkan, perhaps one of the most treasured ancient Mayan monuments, is in the north and surrounded by terraces. Today, only three important buildings still stand: the Temple of the Warriors, the Caracol, and the Temple of Kukulkan. What remains has left fascinating clues to the people who built them as well as many questions about their purpose.

What we do know for sure is that this particular place on Earth, the Yucatan Peninsula, has been the site of human activity for thousands of years. The people who eventually became the Mayan-Toltec civilization began here as hunter-gatherers (10000–3500 BCE), and then, during the Archaic Period (7000–2000 BCE) began to cultivate crops such as maize, beans, and other vegetables and to domesticate dogs and turkeys. The first villages of the region were established, as were temples and the identification of sacred sites.

This period was then followed by the mysterious Olmec Period (1500–200 BCE), considered by historians to be the forerunner of all Mesoamerican cultures and the true ancestors of the Maya. They built cities of stone and brick, most famously along the Gulf of Mexico. However, their highly sophisticated art and sculpture, including the colossus heads for which they are most known, influenced the whole region. Their remaining cultural artifacts reveal signs of shamanic and religious practice. The Olmec left behind extensive ruins so massive that they fueled the idea that giants once inhabited the land. Adding to the enchantment is that there is no record of what happened to them.

Other influences on the Maya came from the Zapotec culture (600 BCE –

AD 800), related to the Olmec, which is believed to have shaped Mayan developments in writing, mathematics, and astronomy and the development of the Mayan calendar. The Teotihuacan Period (AD 200–900), named after the great city of Teotihuacan (just north of present-day Mexico City), impacted Mayan religious culture. Teotihuacan was an important religious center devoted to the Great Mother Goddess and her consort, the Plumed Serpent (Quetzalcoatl), and there are historic links between the Plumed Serpent, the most popular deity of the Mayan people, and Chichen Itza's Temple of Kukulkan. The city of Teotihuacan was abandoned around AD 900.

By the time the so-called Classic Period in Mesoamerica came about the Mayan population was in the millions. An elite class governed them, and the hierarchy chose priests and leaders based on family bloodlines. The top echelon picked the Sun Priests, Diviners, and Seers. The main focus in all rituals was corn, or maize.

The Classic Period, or El Tajin Period (AD 250–900), as archeologists call it, is said to be the time when the Maya perfected mathematics and astronomy. In Mayan culture, warriors and great mythological creatures are featured strongly, as is the notion of the cyclical nature of life, which became the predominant system of belief during this time.

Significantly, Mayan people thought that beneath the earth lay the dark realm of Xibalba (pronounced "shee-BAL-ba" and translated as "place of fear"). This is where the great Tree of Life grew up through the earth, reaching to the heavens with 13 levels. This was the route to paradise, or Tamoanchan ("place of the misty sky"), where beautiful flowers bloomed. The Maya did not have a concept of heaven or hell but thought they would undertake a difficult and treacherous journey toward Tamoanchan that began in the underworld of Xibalba. There was fear of trickery and the possibility that the soul would be destroyed by the inhabitants of Xibalba.

The Maya believed that if they could navigate this dicey underworld, then it would be possible to ascend through the nine levels of the underworld and the 13 levels of the higher world to reach paradise. To bypass such a journey, one could be born or die in Tamoanchan, as a sacrificial victim on the ball court, through war, or through suicide. A special goddess for suicide called Ixtab was there to help. She was depicted in artworks as a rotting corpse hanging from a noose in the heavens. Paradise existed on Earth for the Maya, and they believed Tamoanchan was the place of eternal happiness. Once ascended through the thirteen levels, one ended up on a mountaintop on Earth.

For the Mayans, nothing was ever born or died. Their religious beliefs were inspired by the cycle of nature, which also created their view of the gods and the Universe. This view is also vital to an understanding of the Mayan view of sacrifice, since nothing ever lived or died, but was simply a part of nature and birth and rebirth, like the rising of the sun and moon and the cycle of life.

Sacrifice continued to be a feature of the Mayan-Toltec civilization when the two cultures came together around AD 1000. Folklore tells of the victim being painted blue and taken to the top of the Temple of Kukulcan, where they were cut open in the chest with a flint knife and their beating heart removed as their body was cast down the stairway of the temple. Other stories tell of the sacrifice of young boys and girls. Blood was gathered from their genitals, because the Maya believed such blood was the most sacred and would ensure fertile crops. High society women were also chosen for their blood offering, which would be wiped on the idol or altar. Rivals or enemies who were captured by warriors would be made into slaves or laborers, but elite enemy soldiers were sacrificed. The same fate befell orphans acquired through purchase or kidnap.

These stories are based on artifacts found at Chichen Itza and suggest that no one was allowed in the temple except the priests and those chosen for sacrifice. Both men and women were offered to the gods. Ceremonies and fascinating rituals were central to Mayan-Toltec life, including a strange ball game played on the ball court. The men prepared to play the game in a special building and were separated from their wives and fasted, making daily offerings of their blood for up to a hundred days prior to a major festival.

The Toltec were led by a man calling himself Quetzalcoatl, after the Plumed Serpent, who asserted his power and strength in extreme ways to ensure his reign and control over the people. The Toltec were warriors and builders who came to Chichen Itza from the Valley of Mexico and the city of Tula, and they brought with them knowledge of smelting metal and intricate stonemasonry. A process of acculturation took place between the Maya and the Toltec peoples, and the blending of the two cultures and their spiritual practices is evident in the elaborate decorations on the Chichen Itza buildings, especially the great Temple of Kukulkan.

So what about this mystical temple? What do we know about its construction and purpose? Historians and archeologists believe that the Temple of Kukulkan was built at the center of the sacred site of Chichen Itza. It appears to be constructed for astronomical purposes and is oriented to the sun. The temple has four sides, and on each side there is a staircase comprising 90 steps, rising to a final large step, or platform. The temple rises 80 feet (24 meters) off the ground. Much is made of the fact that there are exactly 365 steps in total, one for each day of the year. What that means specifically is not certain, but most scholars believe that they correlate to the Mayan calendars. From the top of the pyramid, the entire city and surrounding landscape can be seen. Inside, the temple is altogether different. It is dark, the air is hot and moist, and the chambers are claustrophobically small.

In 1932, archeologists discovered a box inside the temple that contained coral-, obsidian-, and turquoise-encrusted objects alongside human remains, giving one of the first clues to scholars that there was much more to this temple than they first thought. Three years later, in April 1935, a stairway was discovered underneath the northern side of the temple. When archeologists dug through from the top of the temple, they found another temple buried below the existing one. It was during this find that researchers concluded an inner pyramid, measuring approximately 108 feet (33 meters) wide and shaped similar to the outer pyramid, was a previous structure. This pyramid had only nine steps and rose to a height of 56 feet (17 meters), leading up to a platform.

Scholars also discovered a second chamber, which they named the Chamber of Sacrifices, because it contained two parallel rows of human bones set into the back wall.

Also found in this room was a jaguar statue, shaped like a throne. It was painted red, with 74 jade inlays for spots, crescent eyes made of jade, and white-painted flint for teeth and fangs. The impressive throne was also facing northeast and had a disc found on the back of it, possibly used for burning incense. Who did the jaguar throne belong to? Did the priests of the temple use it?

No one knows for sure who built the first temple on the site, or why the Mayan created a much larger structure on top of, or in the place of, the first building. So many questions about the temple remain unanswered, and yet another puzzle recently came to light: How much did the early settlers know about the land on which they built Kukulkan?

Scientists have newly discovered an enormous sinkhole right underneath the temple, which currently threatens its very existence and adds to the mystery of the choice of this specific sacred site. The sinkhole is around 82 feet (25m) by 114 feet (35m) and up to 65 feet deep (20m). The river, which runs north–south through the underground cavern, or cenote, could cause the potential collapse of the pyramid. Experts say that it's unlikely to happen for another one hundred years or so, because the layer of limestone is at its thickest about 16ft (5m) by 114ft (35m) and up to 65ft deep (20m) at the place where the pyramid is actually sitting. Cenotes were very important to the Maya culture and are still revered by present-day locals and visitors.

One other suggestion has been made about the discovery of the underground river. Archeologist Guillermo de Anda believes that the temple complex was built according to Mayan cosmology, that the cenotes surrounding the temple of Kukulkan represent points on the compass, and that the underground river connecting them is at the center of the Mayan Universe.

Cosmology and astronomy are central to understanding the secrets of Chichen Itza's intriguing pyramid. At the vernal equinox, on March 20th, and the autumnal equinox, on September 21st, around 3pm in the afternoon, the sun's rays light up the western side of the pyramid's main stairway. It creates one of the most impressive and yet mysterious aspects of Kukulkan, causing seven isosceles triangles to emerge that form the shape of the body of a serpent about 37 yards long. As the sun and the shadow change, the serpent appears to be moving slowly down the pyramid until it meets up with the stone-carved head of the serpent, which sits at the bottom of the stairway.

Researchers suggest that the "symbolic descent of Kukulkan" is connected to agricultural rituals. It's a fascinating aspect of the temple, which has added to its renown on the Yucatan Peninsula and to its place as one of the most enigmatic sacred sites. Is this an accidental phenomenon, or did the builders of the pyramid intend the snake to slide down the balustrade? And where did the Maya get their advanced understanding of mathematics and geometry to create this phenomenon and the amazing temple?

Any description and understanding of the Temple of Kukulkan requires a basic knowledge of the legendary Quetzalcoatl, which, as noted earlier, means "plumed or feathered snake or serpent." Quetzalcoatl is one of the main gods worshipped by ancient Mesoamerican civilizations. Briefly, it is believed that Quetzalcoatl went to the underworld to collect the ancient bones of human beings. When he returned to the surface of the earth, he mixed his blood with the bones of the ancients to create a new race of humans. He then exiled himself from the earth, and his heart ultimately became the morning star. It was believed he would return to the earth.

Aztec legend has it that the legendary Ometecutli, Lord of Duality, and his wife, Omecihuatl, Lady of Duality, were responsible for all life on Earth. They were said to have had four sons, representing the four directions: Quetzalcoatl, Tezcatlipoca, Huitzilopochtli, and Tonatiuh. These sons also became ruling gods.

Quetzalcoatl was considered benevolent and the overseer of agriculture and art. Fighting ensued between him and Tezcatlipoca, who oversaw all evil, sorcerers, and darkness. He is depicted in the form of a tiger. There was so much fighting between these two gods, so much death and destruction that caused humans to be wiped from the earth, over and over again, that they were ultimately banished from Earth by the other gods. Quetzalcoatl became so angry that he caused a great rain of fire to destroy the earth and destroy man one last time. Those men who did not perish were transformed into birds.

All priests in the Toltec cult were given the title of Quetzalcoatl, and one in particular claimed to be the second coming of the original Quetzalcoatl. He reigned for decades and was very powerful but was eventually deposed. He sailed east on a raft of snakes vowing, just like the original Quetzalcoatl, to return to rule again. It is believed that it is his return that is being referenced by the artwork on the temples and by the shadow serpent crawling down the side of the pyramid.

One other interesting aspect of the temple's design is an acoustic feature believed to have been deliberately built into the site. The Temple of Kukulkan is said to "sing"—or rather chirp—just like the call of the long-tailed quetzal bird of Central America and Mexico. Clapping ones hands together in front of the temple creates a strange set of chirping echoes that sweep up the staircase.

Along with this acoustic feature is another. Someone standing at the foot of the temple and shouting will hear their voice come back as a piercing shriek. Plus, if a person stands at the top of the temple and speaks normally, their voice will carry and be heard at the ground level for some distance. The belief that this is deliberately built into the temple's architecture comes from the fact that this same feature is shared by another Mayan pyramid, at Tikal.

Two other mythical tales of the serpent god are important to the story of the pyramid. One tells of a boy, born a snake, who lives in a cave, hidden away from the people. As he grows older, it becomes obvious that he is the plumed serpent. His sister cares for him, but as he grows older he becomes too big for the cave and must leave. His departure from the cave into the ocean causes a huge earthquake. Folklore holds that any earthquakes or tremors in July are a sign by Kukulkan to his sister that he is still alive.

A more modern story tells how Kukulkan was a winged snake who flew to the sun. He tried to talk with the sun, but the sun was prideful and burnt his tongue. Another story tells how the serpent god creates the wind by moving his tail and the rain by sweeping the earth clean.

After an incredible reign, the Mayan-Toltec cities were abandoned during the Post-Classic Period (AD 950–1524). There is no explanation as to why, although there are many theories about the Classic Maya Collapse, as experts call it.

Among the most posited theories is that long periods of serious drought led to mass migration from the cities. Scientists have taken samples of sediment from nearby lakes and caves and have found evidence supporting the idea that severe drought caused people to leave the cities. The sediments show a significant drop in the amounts of rainfall during the years the population demise is said to have begun. Other studies, including one of the tropical cyclones that are frequent in the area, have also shown that cyclone activity was significantly lower than expected for two centuries, between AD 800 and AD 1000—another indicator of drought. Experts also believe that the city of Chichen Itza and the temple complex were almost abandoned during a second significant drying trend and climate reversal, around AD 660–1000. This kind of environmental disaster would have caused competition for food, possible intertribal warfare, and political and social instability.

Among the other suggestions for the decline of the Mayan-Toltec civilization include foreign invasions, a disease epidemic, and famine. It is hard to imagine that such a sophisticated culture, with knowledge of astronomy, mathematics, art, and architecture, would almost completely disappear. Certainly, the climate cycle would have a great influence on this particular region and cause these people to migrate to other areas. For example, the migration stories of the Hopi Indians describe the Mayan-Toltecs as being a part of their mythology. Chichen Itza provides a wealth of information of a time and civilization that still leaves us wanting more.

Spirit Traveling to Chichen Itza – the Temple of Kukulkan

Chichen Itza was both a place of intrigue and trepidation for me. I knew I had several past lives there, and now the time had come for me to spirit-travel to this site. I have to admit to feeling nervous at the thought. My guides, of course, knew all of this. I announced to them that I was ready to face my past. We clasped hands, and rising skyward, flew south. When we arrived, we had time-traveled to 3028 BCE.

The jungle surrounded us on all sides, but we found ourselves in a small clearing where the land was relatively flat. Rocks were scattered around us, and the vegetation was wet and lush. Nearby was an outcropping of rocks with a small opening that was barely visible. Through the dense vegetation of the jungle, we could see a man approaching us. He was ornately dressed, with feathers and a loincloth.

"My name is Aut," he said. "I am one of the high priests of Chichen Itza, and it is my job to guard this site and the Temple of Kukulkan."

The high priest beckoned my guides and me to follow him toward the outcrop, and as we drew closer, we could see that he intended for us to follow him inside the small opening. One by one, we squeezed between the rocks and descended a crude set of stairs. The underground cave opened up before us to reveal a huge cavern with a large pool of emerald-green water. At the far side of the cavern, I could see other openings that looked like they would lead farther into the earth.

"The Mayan people worshipped the serpent called Kukulkan," explained Aut. "In the beginning it was as all unions between the people and their gods. We had respect and fear. His presence was ominous."

Aut spoke in a soft voice. "This underground cavern was here long before the Mayan people arrived. When we discovered this cavern with underground lakes, we met the great serpent Kukulkan."

As Aut spoke the name of the serpent, I thought I saw the shining water stir. Suddenly, there was a flash of silver and gold, and I was transfixed as the mythical creature emerged briefly from the water. The serpent was enormous, and I stared at the lake, hoping the creature would reappear.

I was so intent on seeing it again, I barely noticed the man standing next to me. Startled by his presence, I moved back quickly toward the rock wall of the cavern. The dark-haired man, dressed in a simple cloth wrapped around his hips and a necklace with a single shell hanging from it, raised his hand slowly, calming my alarm. I looked at my guides, who seemed mesmerized by the water's reflection dancing alongside the cavern wall.

The voice of Kukulkan spoke: "I govern all the water on Earth, and the stars are my home." I could feel the air in the room change as he spoke. It was as if every word had such weight and meaning, it literally hung in the air.

"I am Kukulkan, and this is my water," he declared. "My body is that of a serpent, but I also take the form of a man." The priest stood head down in reverence alongside me. I immediately followed his lead, lowering my head while thanking Kukulkan for allowing us to see him and stand near this sacred lake. I thought to myself, *It is no surprise that for thousands of years, the people worshipped this god, Kukulkan.*

"The water in these lakes is the purest found on Earth, and infused with electromagnetic energy from the planet," the serpent-man told us. As he spoke, the water glistened changing from a stunning jewel-like green to a beautiful blue and back again.

Respectfully, I asked him when the first temple was built.

"It was built in 500 BCE, as a means of protecting the opening to the cavern and to harness the energy the priests felt from the sacred water. It was later, in AD 300, that the outer pyramid was built, to further harness the energy of the water and to access the stars," Kukulkan explained.

"The early Mayan culture practiced their ceremonies at the opening to the cavern for thousands of years but did not feel a need to protect the sacred site since only they knew of its existence," he continued. "Various stone structures were placed around the site to signify its importance. However, as the society grew, and other tribes warred against the Maya and challenged their power, the priests believed they must protect its secrets."

Kukulkan went on to explain that the priests also learned of the astronomical significance of the site. "As their culture progressed, and they learned more about their place among the planets and the stars, they created the first pyramid to symbolize that."

Kukulkan turned and looked at the High Priest Aut (for that was his name), acknowledging him and saying: "The high priests of this early culture were the only ones to enter the cavern. I guided them in their understanding of water and earth and taught them about the energy that is created by these two elements. When the priests came to me and told me they wanted to protect the opening of the cavern, I began to teach them about building using specific astronomical alignments and formulas, as well as particular mathematical equations that they could utilize in the construction of the pyramid. Equally important was that it lined up with and corresponded with their calendar."

I asked him to tell me more about the first temple. Kukulkan replied: "It was built for protection, but there were also rooms inside that were used for fertility rights and ceremonials. The Mayans worshipped the sun, water, moon, and sky. Some could turn into jaguars!" He smiled a very small but significant smile.

The serpent-man Kukulkan led us back through the opening. We emerged from the cavern, where he told me: "This is what the priests did each year as a part of the story of emergence into this world. They would crawl out of this cavern through the opening as if they were being born into a new world."

We followed the high priest, Aut, and Kukulkan to the surface, this time entering a narrow passageway. Once again time had shifted, and we were inside the first temple in the year 500 BCE.

The room we entered was dark and High Priest Aut lit a torch. I could see ornate drawings of the Kukulkan and the priests on the wall. Aut led us through another opening that was small, like a door for a child. We ended up standing in a much larger room where I could see an altar with a jaguar and a serpent carved from stone.

"This is where we made our ceremonies and sacrificed people to appease the gods," revealed the high priest. Calmly, I asked him why they sacrificed people.

Kukulkan, who had been standing with us, listening to the high priest, said, "They wanted to give their most precious gift to the gods." He looked sad. He went on, "We never asked for this type of sacrifice. The Mayans insisted on giving up their most precious gift. The human mind is often clouded by hunger and fear." Kukulkan touched the wall of the chamber. "Their bodies were transformed into fish that swam out to sea. Only their bones remain, as their tears became mother of pearl and their hearts the turquoise found in the land."

High Priest Aut took my hand and led us to the opening at the top of the temple. I felt a warm breeze on my face. Time had shifted once again. Now we were standing in the opening of the second temple, the one that we see today. My attention was drawn to my guides, who were focused on the steep stairway to the ground below. At the base of the temple, there were at least ten jaguars sitting at the bottom of the stairs. Aut turned to me, and without any emotion and ignoring my astonishment said, "Those are the other priests. They are waiting to get back into the temple." I slowly shook my head—the sight of these ten sleek black jaguars was amazing.

From our vantage point at the top of the second temple, I could see across the tops of the trees and take in much of Chichen Itza. My attention was drawn by Kukulkan, who was making a sound like a whistle. I listened, and when he was done I asked him what that was for?

"The whistle is a call to all the water beneath us. The frequency brings harmony and balance," answered Kukulkan. I thought about this ancient structure protecting the water below it, and I asked about the construction of the second pyramid.

"The Mayans, like many tribes that have wandered the earth, wanted to understand and access the stars above them. Through this design, they learned how to work with the electromagnetic energy that runs through earth and travels through water. This special site is one of only a few on Earth where the land allows us to work with the earth's energy. The geometric design of the second pyramid allows the energy to build and move up through the center with such acute force that it can shoot right out of the top! The priests knew the water was a conduit that could electrify the structure, and they would experience a type of space travel inside the pyramid," Kukulkan explained.

I looked at him and said, "Space travel?"

"Yes! Water is very powerful. Many beings from the stars use water as a conduit. We gave the priests information about the earth and planetary alignments within this solar system, as well the galaxy beyond. With this information, they could space-travel much in the way you are space-traveling here now!"

My guides smiled.

Kukulkan continued: "The Early Archaic Mayans forecasted many things that would come to pass on Earth. They knew of the demise of their relatives, the Olmec and the Zapotec. They also knew of their own ending, through the creation of their calendar. The Mayan calendar reflected much of the solar journey and transitions, but also dimensional shifts. The dimensional shifts are the part of the Mayan calendar that those trying to decipher it today just cannot understand. The Mayan people knew that the earth and humanity would shift into another dimension. That is why the calendar ended."

I asked the high priest what happened to the Mayan people.

"Over time, they became desperate as the weather changed and drought ensued. Despite the underground aquifer, the priests forbade the people to disturb Kukulkan, the great serpent, and would not use the sacred waters." Sadly he continued, "Instead, they started sacrificing people to appease the gods, because everything at that time was about having plentiful crops and an abundance of water. In the beginning, they would pray for rain and sacrifice a Mayan on the solstices and equinoxes. Over the years, it progressed to the point that, toward the end, they were sacrificing one to two people per day. Part of the frenzy that added to the demise of the Mayan civilization was that there was gambling, political strife, and corruption. Those who didn't starve migrated to other regions."

The high priest took my hand, "We need to move to the ground below," he said urgently. Suddenly, we were airborne, floating from the top of the pyramid to its base. Aut looked at me, "No one other than the priests ever came back down the stairs." Images flashed through my mind of young girls being led up the stairs, never to return.

Movements at the foot of the pyramid brought me out of my visions, and my attention was drawn to the jaguars that were heading toward the base. I was amazed as I watched them take their first step up the pyramid and transform into priests. Aut said, "This is their path, their ritual, and what they do each and every day since the beginning of the Mayan culture."

Once on the ground, we could see the last priest step through the opening at the top of the pyramid. Aut said, "They will do their daily rituals, and pray to the gods."

Now the sky was dark, speckled with stars. Kukulkan looked upward. "This will be the path of the future," he said.

A jaguar walked up to us as we stood there under the night sky, and the priest and Kukulkan both looked at me. Kukulkan spoke, "He recognizes you."

I asked if he was also a priest disguised as a jaguar. They both shook their heads.

Aut spoke first and said with great gravity, "This is not a priest; this is a jaguar."

"You must go with him, as it is an honor to be visited by the old one," echoed Kukulkan.

I thanked them. The high priest and Kukulkan held my hands and gazed deep into my eyes. I felt full in my heart and soul. I turned toward the jungle and followed the jaguar with my guides behind me.

7

The Khafre Pyramid

If you search for the laws of harmony, you will find knowledge.
—Egyptian Proverb

Of all of the ancient sites in the world, perhaps the Great Pyramids of Giza hold the most fascination for people around the globe. Designated one of the Seven Wonders of the Ancient World, The Pyramids of Giza are three pyramids built for the fourth dynasty of Egyptian kings around 2575–2465 BCE. They rest on the banks of the River Nile in northern Egypt and sit upon a rocky plateau. The pyramids comprise the Great Pyramid, called Khufu; the middle pyramid, called Khafre; and a third, named Menkaura. Their names correspond with the names of the kings for whom they were built.

My focus is on the Khafre Pyramid because of the remarkable energy I experienced while spirit-traveling to this site. I found myself asking a lot of questions. Were these kings buried in the pyramids because of the incredible energy they hold? We know that the afterlife is much more important to the pharaohs of the past, but what happened over hundreds of years that would cause Rameses II to wipe out all traces of Khafre? What sort of man was Pharaoh Khafre? What were the politics of his era, and were they behind Khafre's megalomaniac obsession? Who were the people who built the pyramids? Was there another purpose for them beyond burial tombs? How important is it that these pyramids were built on the axis of the north and south poles? My spirit travels uncover answers, but first, I want to briefly look at what we think we know about the Khafre Pyramid to date.

Pharaoh Khafre

In reviewing the history books we can see that the families of the Egyptian kings of the fourth dynasty were an extremely dysfunctional lot. They lived during a time of great prosperity and peace in Egypt. It is understood that Khafre was one of two prominent sons of King Khufu, for whom the Great Pyramid was built. Khufu's best-known sons were Djedefre and Khafre. Djedefre appears to have been power hungry and the killer of one of Khufu's other sons, Kewab, who was the rightful heir to Khufu's throne. Although Djedefre claimed power, he did not live a long time and was succeeded to the throne by Khafre.

Khafre was also known as Khafra. The change in name is credited to the fact that the pharaoh believed that he was the embodiment of the God Ra. It is thought that the name means, "Appearing Like Re" and is a reference to the worship of the sun god. The cult of the sun god Ra was thought to be prevalent at the time of the fourth dynasty and was based in Heliopolis, the City of the Sun.

The ancient Egyptian historian Manetho, who was writing in the Ptolemaic era, claims Khafre ruled Egypt for 66 years, but recent research suggests his reign was probably much shorter than that, at around 26 years. As with his father, Khufu, there appears to be very little actual evidence of Khafre's reign, other than the remaining awe-inspiring pyramids. It's almost as if he and his predecessor have been completely wiped from the records.

Most of the information gleaned about Khafre comes from the historical reports of the Greek historian Herodotus, writing almost 2,000 years after the pharaoh's death. Obviously, those writings have to be read in context, and with the understanding that the Greeks of that time had a poor view of the Egyptians kings and their massive, apparently ego-gratifying pyramids.

Diodorus, a contemporary of Herodotus, also claimed that Khafre was a tyrant and that the people not only suffered under his rule but that of his father, too. Both reported Khafra to be a heretic and cruel despot who kept the temples closed after his father's death, but there is little evidence other than their writings to prove this.

What historians are more certain of is that Khafre had several wives and lots of children—at least 12 sons and four daughters. By marrying his sister, Khafre kept the royal bloodline pure, and subsequent wives kept the production of sons and future successors in hand. Khafre's own maternal line has been a matter of debate. Some think he is the son of Queen Meritites because an inscription has been found in which he honors her, while others argue that he was the son of Queen Henutsen. Whoever gave birth to this king, it seems they were aware of the clear sociological order that needed to be maintained at that time to rule this prosperous region of the world.

Khafre established a royal court at Memphis, and it is from there that he and his family members and chief councilors governed Egypt. Some of these councilors worked as architects and likely helped lead the building projects of the pharaohs. They were also involved in trade and foreign policy, ensuring that the peaceful and prosperous Egypt that Khafre inherited from his father, Khufu, was maintained. It appears that they were successful, since no evidence of any military activity or attacks on the empire has been discovered for that time period. The economic strength and stable nature of Khafre's Egypt undermine previous historical beliefs that he was not popular with his people. It is likely that the reverse was in fact true, since people thrive in the kind of environment Khafre reportedly ruled over.

As already mentioned, according to the Greek historians and subsequent researchers, Khafre's autocratic ruling style meant that his people hated him (although, as I mention above, I doubt this). While his people may have disliked him, it didn't stop Khafre from enlisting their help in building his pyramid and reportedly trying to outdo his father's Great Pyramid. To begin with, he built his pyramid at a higher elevation than his father's and surrounded it with a complex of buildings and all sorts of elaborate statues. Among the statues is perhaps the most famous: the statue of the Great Sphinx.

The Great Sphinx was carved from a rocky outcrop in a quarry beside the causeway that leads to Khafre's pyramid. The face of the Great Sphinx is thought by some to be based on Khafre's features, and is a human-headed lion wearing the headdress of a pharaoh. Not surprisingly, though, there is ongoing debate about the origins of the Great Sphinx and the date of its creation. Early Egyptologists believed that the Great Sphinx was created long before Khafre's reign. Author Robert K. G. Temple proposes that the statue was that of the Jackal-Dog Anubis, God of the Necropolis. He believes that the face was re-carved into the likeness of Amenemhat II of the 12th Dynasty, based on the style of eye makeup and the pleats on the headdress.

The Pyramid of Khafre

The Pyramid of Khafre stands tall. It is five million tons of stone stacked 471 feet high and 707.75 feet at its base on each side. When you look at the three pyramids from a distance, and on ground level, Khafre seems to be the tallest of the three. It is well known that going back as far as medieval times the tombs inside the pyramids have been robbed of many of their items and riches. Also, much of the smooth white limestone cladding that once covered exterior of the pyramids has been taken, shortening their height. At the peak of the Egyptian dynasties, the pyramids are believed to have had a celestial look about them, especially when the sun or bright moon shone on the white smooth stone.

The Khafre Pyramid has seven major features: the pyramid itself, a satellite pyramid, several boat pits, two temples, and the causeway that leads to the pyramid and is flanked on one side by the Sphinx and the Sphinx Temple.

Access to the inside of Khafre's pyramid is through two entrances, one at ground level and the other partway up the structure. The lower one is a passageway leading into the bedrock on which the pyramid was constructed. This eventually leads into two chambers. A ramp connects the two entrances, and off this ramp is a slope leading to the burial chamber, again carved from the bedrock. The sarcophagus, carved from a block of black granite, is sunk into the rock of the chamber. It is not known if Khafre's mummified body was ever in the sarcophagus. Some inscriptions and statues found around the pyramid complex are some of the best evidence that the pyramid was built for Khafre.

Who Built the Khafre Pyramid?

It was long believed that ancient slaves (in some stories, Israelites) were responsible for building the pyramids at the behest of their overseers, the Egyptian royal family. Now, thanks to modern archeological research, we can be confident that, in fact, it was the Egyptians themselves who constructed these amazing monuments. Archeologists have uncovered villages, along with the remains of ordinary Egyptians, who they believe were likely the work force used to construct the pyramids.

The first pyramids in Egypt, such as the Step Pyramid of Djoser, were constructed in 2630 BCE. Around 2590 BCE, the Great Pyramid was built, and the Khafre pyramid followed in 2570 BCE. Ankhhaf, a counselor, or vizier, in Khafre's court, is thought to have been one of the main architects, and that the Khafre Pyramid is an elaborate tomb. History tells us that it took 26 years to build.

Questions remain about the number of laborers that erected these monuments. According to Herodotus, it took 100,000 men, whereas Dr. Heribert Illig and Franz Löhner calculated a total of 6,700 workers. Illig and Löhner believe they were highly skilled craftsmen and artisans, not the historical image of slaves.

Mark Lehner and Zahi Hawass found ancient bakeries and cemeteries on the Giza plateau. Consequently, the Egyptologists believe the work force was much larger than 6,000–7,000 men, and more likely consisted of 20,000–30,000 men. Hawass and Lehner argue that the crews varied in size depending on the time of the year. In the late summer and early autumn, the Nile would flood the surrounding fields by the pyramids, and a large work force would come to Giza to labor, but during the rest of the year a smaller residential crew would be left working on the site. They believed the villagers worked to build these monuments to honor their god-kings, thereby helping them to reach the afterlife. By working for their god-kings, it would also ensure their own passage into the hereafter, and help all of Egypt.

While some of the questions surrounding who built the pyramids, in terms of the labor force, might have been settled by Lehner and Hawass, what still remains puzzling is the underlying question of who designed and was responsible for the architecture of the pyramids themselves. What is amazing to this day is the sheer brilliance of the structural technology and the fact that the stones line up with such precision. The construction of the pyramids was a massive undertaking, and one that we're still examining.

The prevailing image of how the pyramids at Giza were built is one of thousands of men hauling huge blocks of stone up ramps to the structure. A process that would have taken ages to complete. For years, this was believed to be the building process. However, in 2007, architect Jean-Pierre Houdin shattered that view, when he shared his remarkable findings with the world. Following years of research, Houdin determined that the Great Pyramid of Khufu was built in sections from the inside, using a spiral ramp. It's a complicated system, but if Houdin's theory turns out to be correct, then it reveals the sheer ingenuity and brilliance of the Egyptian architects. Where they got their mathematical expertise and knowledge of geometry and archeoastronomy from remains a mystery.

Why the pyramids were built in the middle of the Giza Plateau is yet another debated question. The Giza Plateau sits on top of the Mokattam formation and is separated from the ancient Maadi formation, south of Cairo, by the Nile Valley. The valley itself was important for transporting building materials such as granite and limestone from the surrounding quarries. The Nile Valley of two thousand years ago was different climatically and environmentally than today. Water was far more plentiful, and the landscape was a rich tropical environment. Actually, there was so much water in the Nile Valley that aquifers existed under the pyramids. We know boats traveled almost up to the entrance of the pyramid sites because archeologists found boat moorings around the temples of the Khafre pyramid.

Plentiful supplies of water and fertile land have always attracted human activity, and it seems that in the Nile Valley, water was key to the lifestyles of the Egyptians. Some have even speculated that the pyramids were built on the Giza Plateau, using underground water sources to generate electricity.

Others suggest that the gold capstones believed to be on top of the pyramids before they were stolen were placed there as conductors of electrical energy. Both of these ideas add to the sense that the Giza plateau area has a special "energy" about it.

Furthermore, the special energy of the Giza site, as well as the polytheistic belief system of the Egyptians, suggests that the pyramids were considered more than just tombs. Religion and a belief in magic were merged in the minds of the everyday Egyptian, as well as the royals and upper strata of the society at the time of the fourth dynasty. Their artwork displays a rich culture filled with ritual, ceremony, and magic. Magic was believed to be a force present in the world. It was even personified as a god called Heka.

The main focus of the religion and magical beliefs was on the king and the gods. Khafre, like his father before him, would have held a unique status somewhere between a human and a god. Much time was spent preparing for the afterlife, which might account for the many funerary monuments. The passage of death and the importance of the afterlife were a big part of ceremonial practices, and it's possible that as well as tombs these sites were thought of as healing chambers, transportation portals, and perceived as home to the gods.

Most important, of course, was the worship of the sun god Ra and Osiris, the ruler of the dead and the underworld. There was persistent belief in the supernatural and beings from beyond the solar system. Priests would conjure magic spells, and it's possible that the pyramids were used for magical ceremonies or as sanctuaries. People often turned to oracles and divination for answers to the questions about life, the future, or why certain things had or were happening. They used amulets for protection against evil and for practicing magic. Superstition and magic pervaded the culture of everyday Egyptians, and the kings would regularly consult with priests when making decisions. Elements of history seem to have been deliberately erased, perhaps for superstitious reasons. For example, a large statue of Khafre was found deliberately buried upside down in one of the temples, and historians are still puzzling as to why that would be the case.

One final area of debate is around the archeoastronomy of the site. The alignment of the temples and pyramids at Giza appears to be the result of astronomical observation by the Egyptians. The pyramids point to the cardinal directions with great accuracy. Significantly, at Giza, the pyramids and the Sphinx are oriented to phases of the solar cycle associated with the equinoxes.

The question is, how did the Egyptians line the pyramids up with the cardinal points so accurately? When you take into account all of the issues involved in getting a simple, accurate reading of the cardinal points, you have to marvel at the fact that they are lined up within mere "arcminutes" of a true north–south line. In the 1980s, historians even discovered that the true north–south line aligned with the ascension date of the king, for whom the pyramid was constructed.

Others have noted that there is a link with the constellation of Orion. When examined closely in the sky, with just the major stars showing, you can see the three major stars at the center of Orion's belt. Some scholars, such as Robert Bauval, have suggested that those three stars are represented by the Great Pyramids at Giza. The orientation to the Milky Way represents the orientation to the River Nile. According to Bauval, the pyramids were more than tombs; they were replicas of the Heavens on Earth.

Spirit Traveling to the Khafre Pyramid

It was early morning, and my guides appeared right in the center of my living room and said it was time to go to Egypt. I was thrilled. Egypt was one place I had always wanted to spirit travel. Wrapping a cloak around me, my guides warned that I must stay out of sight, since the energies at the Giza pyramids could be dangerous. When we arrived at the causeway leading to the Pyramid of Khafre, it was the dead of night.

The night was clear and cold, and the monument loomed over us. I whispered to my guides that I was ready, and they took me inside the ground level entrance to Khafre's pyramid. The unusual light emanating from my guides filled the passageway enough for me to see. I had so many questions I wanted them to answer. I moved my hands over the cold stone of the pyramid, and my mind immediately moved to thoughts of Pharaoh Khafre and the political time in which he was ruler.

Suddenly, the passageway filled with the sound of whispered voices, and as I tuned in to listen to them I heard one voice more clearly than the others. It was the voice of the overseer and priest advisor to Khafre, Iunre, who was also his oldest son. He talked of trouble in the lower regions of Egypt. As the voices drifted away, one of my guides explained that there was unrest in the different regions of Khafre's kingdom. Up until this point in history, Khafre and his father had prevented any chance of an uprising in either Upper or Lower Egypt by immediately quelling rebels or those who challenged their overwhelming power.

"Other members of the Egyptian aristocracy were working to overthrow Khafre's family. He was an arrogant man, who ruled with an iron fist. His temperament was similar to that of his father, but Khafre was more tenacious and competitive. He wanted to be the greatest pharaoh that ever lived," my guide explained.

"It had been almost 12 years since Khafre, perhaps due to a continued stomach ailment, had handed over the reins of power to another of his sons, Menkaura. While Menkaura was considered the king, the real power still rested with Khafre. He had many enemies in Egypt who still were determined to overthrow Khafre and his family."

I leaned into my guides and asked in a whisper, "So what happened to Khafre if he didn't die while on the throne?"

"His life ended under the direction of a rival regent, Seneferu-khaf, son of the vizier Nefermaat II and treasurer of the king of Lower Egypt, who had him slain in his own palace in the middle of the night. The murder of Khafre was a clear message to Menkaura about the political direction he was to take."

We took a few steps down the narrow corridor, and I stopped and asked, "How was he murdered?"

"Khafra was given an herbal remedy for his stomach condition, which had developed as he aged. On the night of his death, the remedy was not prepared by his usual physician but instead by Nubhotep, the wife of Nebemakhet, the trusted chief justice and vizier to Khafre. She was a prophetess of Hathor and the daughter of Djedefre, Khafre's brother."

I suddenly remembered what I had read about the dysfunctional history of this family, and as the guide continued his story, it all began to make sense to me.

"Djedefre's older brother, Kewab, was intended for the throne but died putting Djedefre in power. Djedefre married Kewab's widow, Hetepheres II. The undertow of lies and betrayal stick with this family for generations to come."

I asked my guides to please show me what happened, and in an instant, the walls of the passageway opened up. We watched as the murder scene played out like a vision before our eyes.

Khafre, bent and twisted with age and racked with pain, sits on a chaise lounge and orders Nubhotep to bring him a remedy. Khafre hurriedly drinks the remedy, desperate for the relief he thinks it will bring and almost immediately falls unconscious. Seneferu-khaf emerges from the corridor and helps to lift and carry Khafre to his chambers, but while doing so he intentionally initiates a fatal blow to the heart. It is a technique for stopping the heart, learned from the priests who belonged to the cult of Anibus. To others, the strike will appear as if Khafre has fallen hard on the marble floor, and the resulting bruise will give no indication of what has really happened.

The walls of the narrow passageway came back into view, and the vision disappeared. Once more, I was in the bowels of the pyramid. My guides urged us on, farther inside the enormous structure, and I glanced about me, feeling like a spy about to infiltrate the secret lives of this powerful family. We made our way down another long corridor. We moved into a subsidiary chamber and, instantly, the air shifted and became thick and heavy.

The high-pointed ceiling was illuminated, as though an internal light source was present, and I was amazed to see gigantic ancient beings with pale, bluish skin standing in the middle of the chamber. My guides whispered an explanation. This ancient race of giants had lived on Earth for centuries before the time of Khafre. They were the ones who developed this site, giving the blueprints of the pyramids to the people of Egypt and it was their technology that created the sophisticated Egyptian society. This ancient race educated the Egyptians of 12,000 BCE with math and science and taught their process for building with granite and limestone.

An elder stepped forward. This was Tu. His name, he said, was used in different cultures throughout history. Tu described how he was instrumental in the creation of the Egyptian pyramids. As he talked a low hum emanating from the ancients began to fill the chamber. I felt my heart begin to race, and my fear must have been obvious, because my guides pulled me closer. They explained that the ancients were demonstrating how this sacred room was used. The hum became louder and clearly registered the key of D sharp.

Tu looked deeply into my eyes, calming me. The sound filled the space entirely. My legs weakened, and I began to levitate. Tu grabbed my hand. Weightlessness, he explained, is created when sound and gravity mix at a certain vibration. Sound and vibrations created in this chamber during the time of the Egyptians were used for healing and transportation to Orion, the home of Earth's original inhabitants.

We were moving on again, through the pyramid. Tu explained that Giza had always been a sacred place, long before the pyramids were built. In fact, he said the pyramids were built around the site in order to maintain and hold the energy.

"We taught the Egyptians how to use sound chambers for healing and transportation," Tu said. "Orion was home to the Savrock, who helped Earth's people navigate their world. The Savrock were the first to arrive on Earth, and responsible for building elaborate underground tunnels beneath the earth's surface. They were instrumental in ensuring that there was a way back home, and that we built the pyramids. Others came from Orion, including the Egyptian demi-gods, led by Ra. The Orion constellation influenced the people of Egypt for hundreds of years."

We entered the burial chamber. Instinctively, I looked at my feet and realized that they were no longer on the path and that I was still levitating. I had literally floated about a foot (30 centimeters) off the ground. Tu continued to speak. "Inside this burial chamber the dead were ritually washed and dressed and placed in the open box cut from the stone. The crypt was a portal for travel to Orion, and the hum of the ancients was part of the key."

Now my feet were on the cold hard stone, and I started to feel an energy coming down through the top of the pyramid, as if a gate had opened. Once again the air changed, and waves of electric vibrations went through my body.

Tu began to speak again: "The pyramids were built 2,000 years after these chambers were carved out of the earth, 12,000 years ago, and they correlate with pyramids all over Earth. Of course, the pharaohs insisted on burial in these great pyramids. They understood the journey, and wanted to be the first to arrive at the celestial destination, but they weren't buried here. We had influenced the people and left our mark through the construction of these great temples. Unfortunately, it led into war with other ancients because they wanted the power these sites would give them.

"Anibus, who arrived here 7,000 years ago from the Southern Cross constellation, was determined to rule the earth's people. Anibus was thought to be the son of Ra but was, in fact, adopted by Isis and Osiris. He was soon put in charge of the afterlife and all who enter, giving him the power he wanted over humanity. Anibus had a hidden agenda, his ultimate goal was to infiltrate Orion, the home of the Savrock, but first he needed to be in full control here on Earth. However, we had been warned of his plans, and when he tried to travel through the portals he was blocked. The portals were closed on the side of Orion."

As this information was shared with me, I could see Orion's belt, like three shining lights inside the pyramid blinking and floating above me. With all the patience in the world, Tu continued to speak.

"Khafre was buried almost 404 miles (650 kilometers) from here, in the Valley of the Kings. This pyramid, named after him, was built long before Khafre. The family conquered those who held the pyramids before them and took them as their own.

"Khafre was obsessed with having the status of a God and adorned this pyramid with statues he had specifically made for the purpose. Consequently, the Egyptian people became settled with the transition of power and belief that their king was a god. Khafre's people worshipped him, but when he died his body was interred in the Valley of the Kings."

I saw a look in Tu's eyes that seemed far away. He turned toward me and said: "The Savrocks and the other ancients of Orion continued to block Anibus. Eventually, he gave up his quest for domination of the earth and returned to his homeland, vowing that one day he would return."

Tu led me to the crypt carved out of granite, his warm hand still holding mine. I looked at this simple, long box and understood now how the

Pharaohs could believe that this was the passageway to another realm. There were no inscriptions, because this was not ultimately a burial crypt for the Pharaohs.

I realized my guides were anxious to leave. I wasn't sure about the reasons for their urgency, but I followed them as we walked to the doorway. I looked back to thank Tu, but he and the ancient giants were already gone. I hurriedly walked after my guides along the passageway, all the way to the outside of the Khafre Pyramid. I really questioned our current understanding of time and space, so many hundreds of years have passed, and yet these ruins remain solid.

My guides insisted I pull the hood of my cloak up around my head, and they pulled me into the dark shadows created by the pyramid's walls. Several dog-headed men rounded the corner; they appeared to be looking for something. Once they were past, we moved rapidly over the Giza Plateau and then back once more to the safety of my home.

Later, back in my office I had time to reflect on what had happened at Khafre's pyramid. It was interesting to me to learn from Tu of the connection to Orion. I was not surprised that the pyramids were so much older than had previously been thought, or that the inner chambers, as suggested by the French architect, Houdin, were built first and the pyramids constructed from the inside out. However, the Egyptians' understanding of the Heavens above them, particularly the constellation of Orion, was now absolutely clear. The placement of the pyramids at Giza was almost a replica of the night sky under which they lived and hoped one day to return. The Egyptian people understood more than our own history reveals today. They were an advanced people, with a complete understanding of astronomy and engineering.

8

The Rock of Cashel

*Wisdom, peace, and unity flowed down
through the ages from the great rock.*
—Cashel of the Kings

Ireland's rain-swept landscape is dotted with churches, monoliths, and castles—the remnants of a rich and complex history. The Rock of Cashel in County Tipperary, a thousand-year-old relic of medieval Ireland, is one of the most fascinating. It speaks of ancient Ireland and a mysterious time, long before history was recorded. It is known by its Irish name, Carraig Phádraig, and over the years has been called Cashel of Kings and St. Patrick's Rock. The Rock of Cashel is really a collection of buildings and ruins built on a massive stratified limestone outcrop, rising prominently from what has been called the Golden Vale, a huge plain of fertile farmland.

The folklore of Cashel and the surrounding area is filled with stories, including tales of a mysterious people called the Tuatha Dé Danann. One of the most famous describes how the rock came to be. The devil is said to have broken his teeth by taking a bite out of Devil's Bit, a mountain 20 miles (32 kilometers) north of Cashel. The rock that we see today was the result of the devil spitting it out; indeed, the shape seems to fit nicely with the missing tooth-shaped gap that is plainly visible on the skyline on the mountain above.

No matter how this geological feature was formed, it is easy to imagine its significance for early Irish inhabitants as a high vantage point for survey and defensive purposes. Unsurprisingly, the site became a fortified castle (the Irish word *caiseal*, from which Cashel is derived, means "rock fort"), probably as far back as the fourth century.

What can be seen today atop the rock is the ruin of structures built in the 12th and 13th centuries, but it is in the fourth century that historians believe that the Rock of Cashel first became a significant base of power. The kings of the Eóganachta clan used the rock as a center from which they conquered much of the surrounding area of Munster.

In the fifth century, the clan developed links to the Christian church through the influence of St. Patrick (c.432) and his followers. A famous story about the conversion of the king of the Eóganachta clan to Christianity has been passed down through the centuries. According to legend, St. Patrick accidentally stabbed King Aengus MacMutfraich in the foot with his massive walking staff, or crozier. The stabbing pain was so severe, the king apparently believed it to be part of an initiation rite and bore the intense pain accordingly. (He may have also been influenced by the reputation of St. Patrick, who had reportedly taken other more violent actions against nonbelievers.)

The myths and legends surrounding St. Patrick seem to have had a huge influence on people and the stories about the Rock of Cashel. Known by his Latin name, Patricius, or modern Irish name, Padraig, St. Patrick was actually a fifth-century Christian missionary from Wales. He became known as the Apostle of Ireland, as a result of his many exploits and events in Ireland. Much mystery surrounds the man, including the dates of his birth and death. Historians believe he was captured from Britain by Irish pirates and lived in captivity as a slave in County Down, where he was forced to tend flocks of sheep and pigs. After some time, he apparently escaped and returned to Britain and went to study in France, where he became a cleric. Later, he felt compelled to return to Ireland, where he planned to spread the seeds of Christianity, although some say the only reason he made it back into Ireland is that he was actually a slave trader. There are many legends and stories that have passed down through the ages; some—even most—may be apocryphal, but we know that he was incredibly popular and celebrated widely.

In the 10th century, the Eóganachta clan lost their favored location atop the Rock of Cashel to the marauding O'Brien tribe, who were led by one of ancient Ireland's most famous figures, Brian Boru. Eventually, Brian emerged the triumphant victor in Munster and, by uniting regional chieftains, established a very powerful high kingship, which was successful in defending Ireland against the Danes at the famous Battle of Clontarf, in 1014.

The mighty O'Brien dynasty brought peace and prosperity to the people until 1169, when Strongbow arrived with English invaders from the neighboring island. Around the beginning of the 12th century, the Rock of Cashel changed hands again. This time, Brian's grandson, King Muircheartach O'Brien, gave the rock to the Catholic Church, to prevent the McCarthy clan from winning back the site. (McCarthy's ancestors were the original Eóganachta.) The McCarthys eventually moved south to the coast of County Cork, but before leaving, Cormac McCarthy commissioned the building of Cormac's Chapel, as a show of goodwill, in 1169.

The oldest building on the rock is a 90-foot-high (27-meter-high), round tower similar to other towers found in Ireland. Round towers were built, first and foremost, as watchtowers, and as protection from the Vikings. The entrance to the tower was 12 feet (4 meters) off the ground, on the first floor, and could only be reached by a ladder that would be pulled up in the event of an attack. It was built in the dry stonewall fashion of the time (1101), which means no mortar was used (it has since been added as a means of preservation).

Local people, including the Irish historian H. O'Brien, have claimed that towers like this one, which are found across Ireland, were built by the Tuatha Dé Danann, or the People of the Goddess Danu. These people, about whom there is much controversy, are said to have been the inspiration for a wealth of stories that the clans lived by.

Who were the Tuatha Dé Danann? The belief is that they were Irish gods who came from "The Island of the West." Some speculate that the high, round towers in Ireland were used not only for defense but also ceremonies centered on the worship of the sun and the moon.

According to legend, the Tuatha Dé Danann invaded and ruled Ireland 4,000 years ago. They came from a mystical place associated with eternal youth and magic. Scholars say that the Tuatha Dé Danann were named after their goddess, Anu/Anann, but the name may also refer to a king or a place from which they hailed. The Tuatha Dé Danann translates as "tribe of Danu," and were believed to have had supernatural powers. They were considered a race of demi-gods, much like Thor and Odin from Norse mythology. In spite of the defeat at Clontarf, many Vikings and Scandinavian warriors did settle in Ireland and intermarried, to become as Irish as the Irish themselves, so it's no wonder that Norse mythology is prevalent in Ireland's folklore.

Alongside the round tower is the aforementioned Cormac Chapel—an early and well-preserved example of Irish Romanesque architecture. It is unusual because it has twin towers on either side of the nave and chancel. Carpenters from Germany, sent to the chapel by the abbot of Regensburg, decorated the towers. When the chapel was built, it featured many expensive and elaborate decorations and mysterious carvings. However, the intervening years have worn them away, and only vestiges survive. The Romanesque splendor of the chapel can still be found in the detail on the doorway arches and carved vignettes. The oldest and most important Romanesque wall paintings in Ireland remain on the interior walls of the chapel, while the remains of paintings that date from 1160–70 can be seen on the upper walls and vault. The sophisticated renditions of the Nativity found in the chapel suggest that some of the artists were from England or Normandy. Along with a trove of art, the chapel has a small scriptorium, where books were created and stored.

The interior of the chapel is eerily dark. Inside the main door lays the sarcophagus containing the remains of Tadhg MacCarthaigh, the brother of Cormac (who at the time of internment was King Cormac). The tomb is adorned with carvings of snakes that intertwine to represent eternal life. They are carved in the style of typical Scandinavian Urns. Like many places in Ireland, the chapel is said to be haunted; there can be little doubt that the wind whistling through the old ruins, the many gravestones, and the cold, gray sky of Ireland add to the atmosphere of mystery surrounding the chapel and the rest of the buildings and ruins on the rock.

Once established in the area, the Catholics built a cathedral on the rock, between 1235 and 1270. It followed the cruciform pattern (the shape of a cross) and had no aisle, just a central tower. A Gothic structure, it overshadows the other ruins and has a square tower and turret on one corner. The cathedral was expanded several times over the years. In the 15th century, an impressive castle was built that formed one arm of the extended building. It was a residence that now houses St. Patrick's Cross, the 12th-century crutched cross at which the first king of Munster, Brian Boru, and subsequent kings were inaugurated. An adjoining building, the Hall of Vicars Choral, was built 300 years after the first stones of the cathedral were put down. This hall was where choral laymen would assist in the chanting and singing at the cathedral services. The stonework throughout the structure contains what are thought to be mason marks.

History tells us that, in the Middle Ages, Ireland was beset by one invasion after another, as well as fighting among the clans and violence against the Church. Vikings and Anglo-Normans sought to conquer the country and, of course, vanquishing the inhabitants of the Rock of Cashel would put any invader at an advantage.

In 1647, during the Irish Confederate wars, the parliamentarian troops of the English army destroyed and looted much of what existed at Cashel and on the rock. Hundreds of troops and clergy were massacred at the hands of Murrough O'Brien, the 1st Earl of Inchiquinn, a surrogate of Oliver Cromwell and the Protestants. Perhaps it is ironic that an ancestor from the great family that established the rock in the days of Brian Boru was now responsible for its almost complete destruction.

One final blow to any chance that the Rock of Cashel's structures could remain intact was the decision by Protestant archbishop Arthur Price in 1749 to remove the roof of the main cathedral. The archbishop claimed the building could not be reroofed, though many are suspicious of his decision, believing that he chose to create a new cathedral, rather than preserve a site powerfully connected to the legacy of the Irish clans and positively associated with St. Patrick and the Catholic Church.

What was not destroyed in the sacking of the Rock of Cashel was an ancient document compiled by Franciscan monks from an earlier text. It was called the *Annals of the Four Masters* (*Annála na gCeithre Maístrí*), which was written between 1632 and 1636. In the text, monks recorded that the Tuatha Dé Danann, the ancient clan thought to have been responsible for the round tower, ruled from 1897 BCE to 1700 BCE. If true, this raises more questions than answers about this ancient people. There is so much folklore surrounding the Tuatha Dé Danann that many, many people believe they were around for much longer than 200 years. Evidence of their existence is found throughout the country. For example, Brigid's Well, another famous landmark named for Brigid, the daughter of the Dagda of the Tuatha Dé Danann, and a healer, was adopted by the Christians and renamed St. Brigid's Well. In the Middle Ages, the Goddess Brigid was merged with the Christian St. Bridget, and both represent many holy wells. Combining Christian saints and Pagan goddesses and gods was a common practice in the Middle Ages.

In the *Annals of the Four Masters*, the monks wrestled with the question of exactly where the Tuatha Dé Danann—a tall, pale-skinned, red- and blonde-haired race with blue or green eyes—were originally from (a question that remains today). There is evidence that the true Irish race arrived by sea from northern Spain, having traveled from as far away as Indo-European sites. However, the lore passed down through the centuries talks of their origins in four mythical northern cities—Murias, Gorias, Falias, and Finias—which might have been located in Lochlann (Gaelic for Norway).

What's even more interesting is that a poem in the *Book of Invasions* (*Leabhar Ghabhala*), which was compiled even earlier than the *Annals of the Four Masters*, in 1150, describes the Tuatha Dé Danann as arriving in Ireland on flying ships surrounded by dark clouds. It tells of them landing on Sliabh an Iarainn (the Iron Mountain) in County Leitrim. As they landed, they are said to have brought three days of darkness over the sun. This description even had the monks questioning where these people came from.

Over time Christian scholars, who could not make sense of the poem, eventually defined the "flying ships" as sailing ships, which were burnt at sea. We know the Vikings burnt their ships as a funerary practice, and the smoke may have been responsible for creating the large columns of smoke and dark clouds. No one really knows.

One more point of interest (particularly to me) is that many of the mythical demi-gods associated with the sacred sites across Europe have uncertain origins, so we're left with only the oral traditions as a source of history. The suggested origins of the demi-gods leaves much to the imagination. Did they arrive from other realms or literally come from outer space? The Tuatha Dé Danann is yet another perfect example of this unanswered question.

Rocks, stones, and land formations like the plateau that the Rock of Cashel sits upon, as well as the towers that litter the landscape, fascinate geologists, historians, and tourists. Did the ancient Irish people understand the spirit of the rocks and the landscape that the Rock of Cashel sits upon? It seems unlikely, given the amount of detail in the architecture of Cashel and its buildings and the use of stones, that the people would not have had some sensitivity regarding the materials that they were using.

Many stories associated with the history of the Rock of Cashel involve the kings of Munster, as noted earlier, but the heart and soul of many Irish tales are the "little people," the leprechauns. In Irish folklore, they are often depicted as bearded and wearing a coat and hat, with shoes. They are considered magical beings who, if captured, would grant three wishes in order to be freed.

In one medieval tale, three leprechauns drag the king of Ulster into the sea. (Note: Ulster is in Northern Ireland, now politically part of the United Kingdom; the Republic of Ireland, in the south, is a separate country.) The king, in turn, then captures the leprechauns, and as is traditional, is granted three wishes for their release. Some believe that the leprechauns could be a mere folk memory of a race of dwarfs related to the Fir Bolg (the Belgae, from northern Europe, near Belgium today), people who were said to have lived in the region of Cashel before the Gaels arrived in Ireland.

One other interesting link to ancient Ireland is that it is recorded that one of the first kings of Munster, Ailill Aulomon, in the first century AD, was in fact a Druid, a Pagan. It seems obvious that the Rock of Cashel was home to both kings and Druids. The Druids were found throughout northern Europe, and their origins remain unknown. Historians suggest that a Druid gave St. Patrick the land for his first church. In Ireland, it is said that a Druid was able to do everything. They were known for being mathematicians, astronomers, philosophers, and masters of natural science, as well as masters of the supernatural. Merlin trained the chosen Druids at the time of King Arthur. Imagine how powerful a Druid king would seem atop the massive plateau of Cashel, commanding the elements, with an Irish fog swirling about him.

Spirit Traveling
to the Rock of Cashel

My living room suddenly became cold, and I rose from my chair to adjust the heat, only to notice that my guides had entered and were holding my cloak. Before long, we were spirit-traveling through a perishing cold evening. We arrived in the pitch-black dead of night at Ireland's famed Rock of Cashel. The wind was cold, too, and must have blown every cloud from the sky. I was glad I had my cloak. The moon was up and shone down brightly on the ruined structure. It seemed larger in the dark and loomed over us. I realized we were standing in the graveyard near the round tower.

Immediately, I saw a ghost, a short fellow who had a sturdy stature and dark brown hair. His cloak and tunic were of high quality, and he stood firmly in his leather boots. I realized that this must be the king of Munster, Ua Briain. He didn't notice my guides and came over to me in a grand manner. He began to speak in a dark, sonorous voice. He was direct and pressed the moment with urgency.

"It is with great regret that I gave Cashel to Patrick and the Church," he said.

I realized that he knew this iconic man, St. Patrick, by his name, and not as a saint. He went on to tell me that he had a spiritual experience with Patrick that led him to doubt his knowledge of the old ways.

He took a deep breath and, in that moment, reminded me of one of the dwarfs from Snow White. "Patrick was a crafty fellow. He may have been a man of the cloth, but he used his position to manipulate others and weave a spell around them to get whatever he wanted."

Clearly the ancient King now believed that Patrick used some sort of magic to persuade Ua Briain to release Cashel to the church. Then he puffed up and burst out exclaiming that Patrick wanted the great Rock of Cashel because he knew it was a place of immense power. "I knew the ancient stories of the Druids and tales of magic at Cashel. I have witnessed many strange things here," he exclaimed.

Ua Briain went on to explain how he believed that the "magic" or "energy" held at the Rock of Cashel would return to the site if he redeemed himself in the eyes of God.

The king admitted that he now understands that Patrick wanted control over the energy of the site in the name of the Christian god. "It was a dangerous bit of business, but I learned my lesson, and here I stay, keeping watch and listening to the likes of them."

I followed his pointing finger. In a wide sweeping motion, the ghost king drew my attention to the other ghosts of kings past, standing among us in the graveyard. They were listening to us.

Leaning toward me, Ua Briain whispered, "We still argue over this place."

I told him that I was sorry for his loss of Cashel, and that I knew that St. Patrick must have had a good heart, as he influenced so many people to do good, long ago. Unconvinced, he smiled and said knowingly, "I was beguiled by that very charm, and I am still not happy about it."

My guides began to walk toward the cathedral wall. It was clearly time to move on. I turned and thanked the once king of Munster for talking with me, and I watched him walk back toward the tower.

The cathedral wall loomed high into the night sky, and I saw another man standing before me. He was slight with brown hair and large brown eyes. It was St. Patrick. Immediately, he began to explain, as if he had heard every word uttered by Ua Briain.

"I am just a humble man who wanted peace for this land. I felt the Church could do that for the people. I didn't understand the extent of the energy that existed at Cashel. There is a magic that is unexplainable all over this island; this is something that the Church understood but was always afraid of."

I watched him look over my shoulder, as if expecting Ua Briain to show up. Nervously, he went on, "I only had in my heart the pain and strife the people had felt through war and untimely battles, and thought this place would bring peace."

I asked him if he had cast a magical spell over Ua Briain, so that he would give up the Rock of Cashel. Almost at once he leaped into the air, as if weightless, and throwing his arms skyward exclaimed, "Good heavens, no! That silly man believes everyone is casting spells over this land and his beloved Cashel. My heart really was with the Church and its growing power over Ireland."

Then in a whispered lament he said, "I had only ever meant to bring the magic at Cashel to the Christians. I realized not everyone had the same vision I did, and greed was a much higher priority for the Church." Then he turned and blessed me for coming to see him and, as he stood before me, he looked deep into my eyes and said, "My heart is true."

I was touched by his words and graciously thanked St. Patrick for talking with me. I asked him to join us as we toured the site, but he whispered something about the chapel and praying and, suddenly, he vanished.

We started to move toward the tower, but my legs felt as if they were stuck in a bog. The hair on my neck stood high, and I felt a presence standing behind me. I whirled around to see an enormous woman surrounded by fireflies that illuminated her whole body.

She introduced herself as Brigid, daughter of Dagda, and one of the Tuatha Dé Danann. I knew exactly who she was! I told her I was honored to meet her. Her voice was deep and smooth, like the rivers that wind through the landscape. She had blonde hair, green eyes, and a strong smell of musk. I found myself feeling woozy, hearing her voice and feeling her energy weave about us like a warm blanket. We entered the tower, and Brigid began to talk.

"We, the Tuatha Dé Danann, arrived around 3000 BCE in Ireland. We are a race of beings brought here by giants. To some we are demi-gods, because our bodies are large like them. We come from the same dimension as the Devic kingdom, a world that is not a part of your cosmology."

Finally, I knew I was about to hear the truth about the mysterious Tuatha Dé Danann. "Giants have roamed the earth in years past," she said. "They had their own magic and the ability to bring us across the border from the world of the Devas to this world. The giants wanted our power, so we hid from them in the landscape of Ireland. That is why many of the Tuatha Dé Danann are named for the hills and water."

Her eyes became wide, as she made to reach across the landscape as if she was touching it.

"The Tuatha Dé Danann protected the Little People of Ireland, as they were our allies. They helped us keep the giants distracted, following false leads. The giants eventually left this land in search of other magical elements that would give them more power."

I asked her if they, the Tuatha Dé Danann, were the fairies that have been talked about throughout the history of Ireland. She wrinkled her nose and said, "Well, this is what the history books may have said, but here is the truth. We are relatives of the fairy folk. Our tasks are quite different. The fairies were in charge of all living things—granting good health, easy childbirth, and an abundance of crops. They are a sensitive group and the caretakers of the Devic kingdom. The Little People, or Leprechauns, had been on Earth long before the giants. They are the caretakers of the ley lines [mystical alignments of landmarks] around the globe. They are a hard-working bunch, who have gone deep underground to preserve their own culture."

A storm seemed to cross Brigid's eyes as she went on to explain, "The Tuatha Dé Danann came to Ireland against our will. We decided to stay to protect the Rock of Cashel and other powerfully magical sites around Ireland. Many people do not understand the power that the earth holds and sites like this one at the Rock of Cashel."

I blinked and, suddenly, we were standing inside a tower that was wide and short, similar to those found in Persia. I looked out the doorway and could clearly see that nothing else remained on the plateau. I realized then that we had traveled back to the beginning of the Rock of Cashel.

"This land at Cashel was sacred and the plateau was the ceremonial ground for the Druids. They came here to build the sacred fire in the first tower that existed in 2000 BCE." Brigid smiled and said, "We were already here and happy to help the Druids."

I watched her gesture to the heavens. She described the Druids' spiritual practice that corresponded with the cycles of the sun and moon. "These yearly markers were used for Druid ceremonies. They knew the sacred energy of each element became more powerful as they neared the Equinox and Solstice. The Druids needed to survive and with what they understood at that point in time they would not have lived on. So we taught the Druids our magic. They were respectful and demonstrated how they had come from a lineage that went further back than our arrival. The ceremonies they practiced dated as far back as 4000 BCE."

Kneeling down, Brigid gathered soil and leaves in her hands, holding onto them while she continued to talk. "The Druids worshipped our presence. They gave names to the land in our honor. Spiritual altars were built and cared for to invoke our spirit. We gave them ceremonies to enrich their connection to the soil, water, wind, and fire."

Brigid then leaned over and put the soil she held back on the ground. She went on, "The Druids learned the transforming energy of the element of fire when combined with the energy rising out of the earth like microwaves."

Inside, I could see a fire pit. Brigid nodded, as she watched me survey the room. "This is where they would build the sacred fire."

I could see a stone slab sitting on wooden posts in the middle of the room. I recognized the granite rock and asked her if it came from the plateau? "Yes," she said. "Many of the stone tables were from this plateau. When the giants summoned us to the Rock of Cashel, a stone slab just like this one was used as a doorway. The element of the granite and the magic of the giants created an opening into the very realm we come from."

She gathered us around the table and said, "The Druids would gather around the stone table and place their seeds for planting on top of the granite slab. They would hold their hands over the fire, capturing the element without burning themselves. With cupped hands, they brought the element to the stone table where their seeds and beans lay. Then they spread the fire over them. The microwaves would rise with such energy from the earth that it would make the seeds and beans dance about the table. The Druids then asked the earth to multiply the seeds, and they would sprout and multiply right before your eyes!"

I watched as the ceremony she was describing happened in front of me. I kept looking for something under the table that would be the cause of all the activity, but there was nothing but the ground. Brigid looked at me and said, "This was our way of helping the people produce plentiful crops and feed themselves."

She then took a gold piece. She laid it on the stone. I watched it literally split in half, like a cell dividing, producing a second piece of gold. This was alchemy at its best!

I asked her if this was where the popular saying about "a pot of gold at the end of the rainbow" came from. She said, "Yes. Cashel was considered the end of the rainbow by the Tuatha Dé Danann."

My mind raced with the stories of leprechauns from Irish mythology. I remembered reading that the Irish of the sixth century believed gold was under the trees. They would tie a scarf around the trees that bore specific markings.

Brigid interrupted my thought, "Trees were used as the legs of the stone tables. Over time, the story of this ancient alchemy was lost. The interpretation of what was once the conduit of this alchemy became the focus of the energy, with the people consequently believing the gold was under the trees." My mind was blown.

The room was filled with electricity and heat from the fire and alchemy stone. Brigid continued to talk.

"The Druids' towers were squatty and short. They built them to signify energy and ceremonial sites across Ireland. Once the clans took over, the shape and size of the towers changed; they became taller."

I suddenly became aware of my surroundings yet again. The tower morphed and changed into the ruin that now stands today at the Rock of Cashel. I noticed that Brigid had moved across the room from me, and touching the walls of the tower she began to speak again.

"This tower was built in 35 BCE. Much of the Druids' old ways was lost. They had become more of a secret society that had to be protected. Only the early kings of Munster knew the alchemic practice of the Druids, and some could replicate it. Over time, this display of electromagnetic energy kept the beans and seeds moving about the stone slab table. The ability to multiply themselves, however, was lost."

Brigid looked away and said, "The kings of Munster knew the old stories of this plateau and wanted to harness the power of the Druids."

I asked her if the Tuatha Dé Danann tried to stop the kings.

"Yes, we tried to stop them, but they became greedy and fought over many sites that held magic," she said. "We made sure the opening to our world that the giants created would never be known, even by the Druids."

Brigid turned toward the door. She looked back at me and said, "The clans revered us and asked us for our help, building these towers higher, reaching for the stars. They thought the magic of the Rock of Cashel came from the Heavens, but we knew what was once a powerful legacy was no more."

My guides led me through the doorway to the outer walls of the chapel. Brigid followed. I asked her about St. Patrick and about his giving Cashel to the Church.

"St. Patrick wanted peace between the people. He understood how powerful this place is. He had suffered in life and knew how many others suffered, too. Patrick believed if the Church had ownership, they would manage its power. He did not understand that the energy here was not to be used the way the Church intended," Brigid explained. "When the archbishop removed the roof from the cathedral, he proved that to be true and turned people away from Cashel. The archbishop believed Cashel was evil and the work of the devil."

I asked Brigid about the story of St. Patrick, in which he is said to have cast out the devil from a cave by removing a large rock that landed at Cashel. Brigid turned to look at me. Her gaze grew sharp, and I could clearly see the details of her lashes and bright, piercing, green eyes.

"St. Patrick did indeed remove a demon from a cave, but no large rock was thrown out, creating the Rock of Cashel. In fact, it was the Tuatha Dé Danann who helped St. Patrick expel the creature. The same electromagnetic energy came from Cashel and arched to the cave, helping St. Patrick remove rock and stone to get the demon out. Patrick was afraid. He thought that only the Church could manage energy such as this. His disposition to the Church caused him to shy away from learning more about the earth's gifts."

Her story made me realize that she wanted to be clear about St. Patrick's misinterpretation of the earth's energy.

Brigid leaned against the chapel wall and said, "St. Patrick died lying on his back in a field of heather. He was praying. Patrick was a good man who left Earth, returning again, like a guardian angel, to the people, to help the poor, sick, lost, and enslaved."

My guides and I looked at each other. Now we knew how St. Patrick and Ua Briain's misunderstanding of intention, land, and spirit had come between them. No doubt, fear was pervasive during ancient times, but I wondered why Brigid thought that St. Patrick, a man of God and faith, would also be so clearly afraid.

"With all power comes fear," she said. "The earth offered so much to the people of ancient Ireland, in terms of powerful energy sites such as this one. The towers once stood, and some still stand, as markers of the sites; the magic was prolific back then. Superstition comes from a lack of understanding. Death, and fears of death were rife, and people created belief systems and rituals that created more fear. They also misunderstood the true power of the earth."

Brigid rose. She was now taller than when I had first laid eyes on her.

"The Tuatha Dé Danann and the fairies guided the people and helped them with all aspects of life. The legends that were passed down through the centuries about magic stones and the Druids left people fearful because, as they are passed down through generations, the true meaning of the stories is lost."

She looked down and continued. "St. Patrick brought new thinking, along with Christianity and a belief that Paganism was the work of the devil. The old ways of spiritual practice began to die out as Christian belief in Heaven and Hell took precedence and people conformed to the new religion. Consequently, a misuse of energy prevailed, and the Tuatha Dé Danann had to move deep underground."

I asked her about the earth, and how it was being cared for since these ceremonies were lost.

Brigid said: "The Little People inhabited the underground caves and tunnels. They managed the earth's energy without being seen. The fairy forts remained for several centuries, but have been disturbed or completely taken down, due to the progress of man and a total disconnect from the old ways."

I wondered if the fairies still existed on the plateau of Cashel and asked Brigid if this is so.

"They are everywhere but no longer revered the way they were in the past," she said. "We are not able to access much of the earth's power anymore. Mother Earth has been depleted. The fairies remain hidden but bless those who do the rounds."

I asked what she meant by "doing the rounds."

"The rounds is an old ceremony ensuring healthy crops, livestock, and good health for one's family. Once again it is a ceremony involving stones. Long ago, people circled a huge stone engraved with markings from years past. As they circled the stone, they would carve their prayers and hopes for the coming year into the stone."

I told her that I knew some people still practice this ancient communication with the stones today.

Finally, we walked together through the grounds, skirting graves. We stopped near the wall that surrounds the Rock of Cashel. I asked Brigid what the purpose of this place was, if it was to only end up in ruins.

"The energy rising from Earth was one of the greatest gifts to mankind," she said, with a hint of sadness in her voice. Then a faint smile passed over her face, "It was glorious while it lasted."

I thanked Brigid and told her that I planned to return to investigate more sacred sites around Ireland. She nodded her approval. Then like the mist that moved over the plateau, she was gone.

My guides took my hands, and we went through the mist to greet the morning sun as it rose in the east.

Conclusion

'Procession Panel', near Bluff, Utah

*As long as we keep looking for the similarities in all of human
history, and stick with what feels comfortable, we ignore the
chance to pursue unconventional ideas and possibilities;
in other words, to go where no man has gone before.*
—Sonja Grace

I am grateful for my gifts as a healer and spirit traveler, and for the ability to receive extraordinary information about what originally happened at these ancient sites—to learn why they were built, by whom, who used them, and what for. My unique conversations with the souls who stay behind and the demi-gods who came to Earth and left, while appearing fantastical, are to me a genuine source of historical information, just as rich as the bones and artifacts that archeologists dig up. From my point of view, my findings at these sites are just as legitimate, grounded, real, and as substantial as any archeologist's, historian's, or scientist's discoveries.

Let's face it, the known history is constantly being altered and revised due to new findings, which overturns evidence previously thought to be watertight. As Graham Hancock has stated, "History just keeps getting older." Spirit traveling to centuries-old monolithic sites and sacred places has opened my eyes to a greater world, one that not only existed thousands of years ago on Earth but also extends way beyond our own galaxy.

My spirit travels have shown me that human history is quite different from what we think we know. In fact, our evolution has been more dependent on the grace of demi-gods, or star beings, than we would ever understand or dare to acknowledge. Hagar Qim, Stonehenge, Kukulcan, Tiwanaku, and the Great Pyramids would not be standing without the technical genius that they, the demi-gods, shared with humankind. We continually marvel at how these buildings came to be, yet refuse to grant even the slightest bit of credence to the possibility that humans had help from something greater than ourselves. I have repeatedly argued that humanity is in a constant state of amnesia, perpetuating the illusion that we evolved solely by accident. Nothing could be farther from the truth, as I know it.

Let's start right at the beginning. *Why* do people experience a "feeling" when they visit these sacred sites? What is it that causes the hair to rise on the back of necks and on arms when touring ancient monuments? Where does that sensation in the gut, that "knowing" that leaves an impression on the heart and mind, really come from?

It is possible that people may be detecting a cataclysmic event that occurred in the very spot they're standing that caused the souls of the distant past to stay behind. Or they may have been drawn to the site because they're connected by past-life experiences, or they are so pulled to these portals and the magnetic energy they still emit today that they feel they just have to go there at least once in their life. Whatever it is, the feelings we resonate with at these sites are undeniable for the "sensitive" human being.

It has become absolutely clear in my mind from my spirit travels that all of these sites had spiritual significance identifiable on the land long before the structures were ever built. Not only the magnificent megaliths but also those sites where spiritual events took place, such as at St. Winefride's Well. Why was Stonehenge built next to Salisbury Plain? What was it about the Island of Malta that inspired more than a half-dozen megaliths, including the magnificent Hagar Qim to be built? What drew the monks to Skellig Michael, such an inhospitable place to build and live? I learned that not only did the demi-gods understand the magnetic energy of the sites but also recognized that all of these sites had portals, and they used them and taught ceremonies to the humans that lived there, based on those energies.

At the end of the Ice Age, 12,000 years ago, portals opened up all over the earth. The portals signaled to the Milky Way galaxy, almost like a phone call to the demi-gods, that Earth was about to start a new phase of humanity. From the beginning, star beings have always been a part of the creation process here on Earth. These intelligent beings have participated in the evolution of humans, and humans have worshipped them for their benevolent guidance. The portals are like worm holes, and they are the means of transportation for the star beings.

These portals still exist in places like Stonehenge, Tiwanaku, The Great Pyramids, The Temple of Kukulcan, and even St. Winefride's Well, although the energy has waned over the centuries. However, in my experience, some sites in the world still have these portals open, and they are still fully charged.

According to quantum physicists, the Universe is in a constant state of co-creation that is made up of bits of information rather than matter. Consequently, some portals are meant to receive information rich in cosmic energy; others are meant to transmit earth energy, which is also filled with information; and some portals exchange both. The demi-gods understood this and utilized the earth's gravitational force almost like an information superhighway, in order to receive information and to travel to and from their planets.

The gravitational force, which is made up of waves that travel throughout our universe, like lanes on a freeway, carries information and other forms of life back and forth. The "gravitational field" is different from the "magnetic field," and is measured in neutrons per kilogram. "The field" is the space around a radiating body or mass, within which the electromagnetic oscillations can exert a force on another like body or mass that is not in contact with it.

One more factor to consider about these sacred sites and their location on the planet is how the buildings tend to line up astronomically; in other words, the builders were looking to the night sky when they laid out their buildings.

When we turn back the hands of time and view the sky as it was in 8000 BCE, we can see what the people were viewing and creating monuments to all over the world. For example, the Pyramids of Giza are clearly aligned astronomically with Orion and the portals that exist there. Looking down on the Great Pyramids from above, it is easy to identify their alignment with Orion's belt. The construction of the pyramid at the Temple of Kukulkan was influenced by the same star constellation as that of the Great Pyramids. Orion's star travelers were very influential on Earth. They left their signature in many structures around the globe that have an obvious specific alignment to Orion's belt.

Other sites, such as Stonehenge, are aligned with the stars as well as the solstices and the equinoxes. The Pleiadians come from a star cluster that is clearly reflected in all of the megalithic monuments throughout the United Kingdom. When I spirit-traveled to Stonehenge, the Ancient Ones defined Stonehenge as one of the main portals to and from the Pleiades. What is yet to be revealed is the much larger henge that exists on Salisbury Plain and is connected to Stonehenge. When finally revealed, it will show us how large the portal really was.

We know unequivocally that ancient cultures used the seasonal cycles of the sun, moon, and stars to navigate and to construct their monuments. Everything that they built had purpose, down to the very last stone. Their knowledge of the cycles of the sun, moon, and stars was profound, and they used it, along with their mathematical brilliance, when building these magnificent structures to map the calendar of the seasons.

A perfect example of this is the complexity of Hagar Qim. Not only its structure but also the evidence of the solstice and equinox alignment tell us that whoever built it came from an advanced culture. During my spirit travel, I toured the site with Pirme'aya. She showed the clockwise circular motion of the temple and how each section reflected different times of the seasonal calendar, reflecting their understanding of the passage of time and the position of the sun during the seasons.

What's even more intriguing about the sites to which I spirit-traveled is that, whether created a hundred or thousands of years apart, the same ingenuity of architectural design is apparent. As I have said many times, that clever design suggests a much higher intelligence was behind the construction, at least much higher than we have been willing to previously acknowledge. The way in which the stones are accurately cut and placed at the Khafre Pyramid, Chichen Itza's Temple of Kukulkan, and Hagar Qim forces us to rethink the commonly held belief that these builders were of a primitive culture.

Although the Khafre Pyramid and the Temple of Kukulkan were built thousands of years apart, the methodology was similar and just as complex. As I learned on my spirit travels, they were built in stages, and not from the outside in but from the inside out. The demi-gods I met explained how they taught humans and shaped the culture and people of the sites, as well as creating these amazing monuments.

The pyramid of Khafre was built using 5 million tons of stone stacked 471 feet high, and historians continue to argue about the technique, time, and manpower it took to build. Why, though, do they resist the idea that humans may have had help, and that those carvings and statues of gods we see today among the artifacts found at the sites were actually in physical form thousands of years ago? Perhaps it's possible that the engineering and mathematical equations required to construct such a sophisticated monument were passed down from these star beings, and that it was they who ultimately enabled mankind to create them.

The other aspect of the construction process the star beings brought with them is that there was an alteration of energy, specifically the use of the gravitational field to assist in the moving of the stones and lifting of them into place.

At Hagar Qim, the builders used shallow canals with large roller balls lined up, two by two, to move the stones across the landscape, clearly an ingenious idea. However, at the same time, the star people of Atlantis were also assisting in moving the megaliths onto the rollers and guiding them into place, again using the gravitational field.

A similar force was at work at the Khafre Pyramid. While we have always been taught that slaves using ropes dragged the stones across the desert, we have been limited by our imaginations, unable to see what really took place. Star beings taught the people how to cut the stones and move them, using technology we do not understand today. Male artisans learned this cosmic technology and cut the stones with great precision, but the stones were moved by a whole other methodology.

While there was certainly some brute force involved in moving them, many of the stones were placed using levitation or gravity manipulation, which was accessible due to the magnetic field that existed at the site during this time. Much in the same way that we lift off the ground in a helicopter, or a plane takes off, or a hover board works, they had technology to lift giant stones from one place to another. The chosen priests of these high temples had been taught the technique for moving the stones around inside the inner chamber of the pyramid. There were many things they could accomplish through accessing that cosmic energy, because this was a portal.

An intelligent, otherworldly force was ultimately the one that created the ancient Egyptian people and their culture. In fact, the ancient cultures of the world were taught by many sophisticated groups of star beings, whose influence is evidenced by the elaborate methodologies used to build pyramids, temples, and megalithic sites the world over. What these ancient people saw in Tiwanaku, Stonehenge, and the Giza plateau was normal to them but far beyond our own imaginations or willingness to comprehend. This really isn't a secret; there are obvious clues left behind in these buildings and the art of each culture, but in many cases, we have been too blind to see it.

Obviously, something was stirring in the world energetically around 8000 BCE. The significance of this time period is represented by the structures and monuments found on the Island of Malta and in Egypt, for example. These countries are only 2,000 miles (3,200 kilometers) apart, yet something big happened in both places that resulted in the complex constructions we see today. Likewise, farther north, in the United Kingdom, on Salisbury Plain, the people were making their way to an energetic site that would house megalithic stones erected over 4,000 years later.

Some of the monuments at these sacred sites boggle the minds of today's visitors. They symbolize the energy at these portals, and the demi-gods who came through them to bring humankind together—to teach them, help them evolve, and ultimately to cross-pollinate. Originally, these sites may have been simple wooden arbors that grew in complexity, but what remains today—the temples, pyramids, and stone monuments—represents a time when these sacred places were charged with a super energy that lasted for thousands of years.

Stonehenge is perhaps one of the best examples, beginning as it did with simple wooden structures, as I witnessed in my spirit travel. Although what remains today is magnificent in its mystery, I am certain that there was once much more complexity to it.

When I physically traveled to England to visit Stonehenge, I met a man who had recently been on an archeological dig at Salisbury Plain. I had learned during my spirit travel that Stonehenge had been a powerful portal for hundreds of thousands of years, beginning, as I mentioned, around 8000 BCE. I was fascinated to learn from this researcher that they had found the tooth of an Oryx, an animal that is a cross between an elephant and a cow. This finding, he informed me, was highly significant and changed all the dates in the history books, putting Stonehenge's creation at around 4000 BCE. He was of the opinion that my dates and my belief that Stonehenge was even older than first thought were spot on, and that the history books would have to be rewritten.

The earth's magnetic field, also known as the "geomagnetic field," begins from inside the earth and moves outward, where it meets the solar wind, a stream of charged particles driven by the sun. When there are solar flares, we all feel it here on Earth, as well as cosmic rays, which come from our galaxy and beyond.

Each of these phenomena impacts Earth, and every living creature on it. These sacred sites have an energetic component that involves magnetic energy coming up through the earth. The microwaves that affected the seeds at Cashel and the magnetic charge at Skellig show us the earth has changed during this particular phase of humanity. Where did the energy go? Why do we not experience these phenomena anymore?

By taking natural resources from the earth, we weaken the planet's energy field. The gemstones, oil, natural gas, and coal are all sacred elements of Earth. We use them because we are intent on survival, but to the point of greed. Back when this phase of humanity began, around 12000 BCE, the earth was rich in natural resources. Now there are great gaping holes and open pockets that deplete it in much the same way they would if someone were to harvest your blood and tissue. The star beings, or demi-gods, taught humans how to utilize this earth energy. We practiced this in ceremonies and rituals. We felt the earth as a living being. This changed with the industrial revolution and, gradually, we've become less dependent on the earth's natural cycles for food and survival.

The time-space continuum has shifted as we near the end of the transition from the fourth dimension to the fifth dimension and into a much higher vibration (for more on this, see my book, *Become an Earth Angel*: Findhorn Press, 2014). We are now living in the fifth dimension, and as a species, we are experiencing time in a completely new way.

In my spirit travels, I was very aware of traveling back through time into the fourth dimension while exploring these sacred sites. The energy within these portals during the beginning of this new phase was more powerful than what I would feel if I were at these sites today. Some of the portals remain more open than others. In some cases, people have tried to rob the energy of these sites, subsequently closing them down. Humans are childlike, in that they need a schedule, boundaries, and a purpose. This is why the demi-gods gave us ceremony. Ceremony had connected us to the cosmos and the earth and directed our curious nature to the higher purpose of this new phase.

Healing and ceremony are at the heart of these sacred places. Stonehenge was used for fertility ceremonies, and the giant stones were supercharged with the cosmic energy of the portal. The folklore surrounding the Rock of Cashel is filled with a belief in magic, and the rock was a ceremonial place dating as far back as 2000 BCE, long before the castle was built.

Clearly the influence of the magical Tuatha Dé Danann was present at Cashel and Skellig Rock. Both sites are rich in mythology. Druid practice was guided and shaped by the ancient demi-gods. The monks of Skellig Rock settled on the island so that they could follow the ancient legends of the Druids and their teachers. They built their beehive huts in AD 500, not only to create shelter but also to create the shape of the womb, representing the earth and all that is sacred in life. This is equally true of Hagar Qim. The energy of these sites drew the people to them so that these monuments could be built and ceremonies could be performed, with the guidance and direction of the demi-gods.

I have come to appreciate that all of the sites visited in this book while spirit traveling were built and used for some type of ceremony. The rituals of El Castillo at Chichen Itza were based on the reverence for the demi-god Kukulkan. The people worshipped the water, sun, and rain. The same is true at Hagar Qim, with altars lined with statuettes and the people worshipping the Goddess, Earth, and the feminine principle. The ceremonies of Stonehenge were also based on fertility and echo the same practice created thousands of miles away in Tiwanaku.

Ceremony is an innate part of the human experience, whether we walk outside and greet the sun or we go to a specific place, temple, church, or synagogue to experience a ceremony that reflects our beliefs. The spiritual experience at these particular sites was so overwhelmingly powerful that the demi-gods and people created structures that would house the ceremonies and influenced the culture for centuries to come.

As humans, we are in sync through spiritual connection—a connection that happens to be infinite because, as souls, we have always been, and will always be. Our orientation to God or Source is a mystery every time we incarnate into physical form. This deep state of amnesia is an aftereffect of our high vibrational soul body entering dense matter. Through lifetimes of this experience, we continue to grow; some faster than others, but all with an effort to evolve the human race—which, as I have learned, is why the demi-gods came to Earth to begin with.

People of today demand proof in order to believe what is being presented to them. We don't ask ourselves what we feel, but rather step into the intellect and insist on a more mental process. I understand my methodology is quite unusual, but so is science until it is proven correct, re-proved years later, then completely redefined a century later. We limit ourselves as to what we are willing to believe may have taken place in the past—all the while creating stories and movies that spring from a wealth of imagination that had to come from somewhere.

Where does the imagination come from? In my humble opinion, it is the soul body—that inner resource that has full access to the hall of records and all that has been and all that will be. When we imagine ourselves feeling good, we usually manifest exactly that: we feel good. When we imagine something scary in the room, we can get pretty worked up, feeling it is almost real. The mind is powerful. It can be a window to the soul, accessing what is real and what exists in other dimensions.

Intellect versus imagination falls short when it comes to what is real and what isn't real. To me, there is no defining line as to what we perceive as real and what is unseen. When we truly understand the complexity of the cosmos, our comprehension of what has taken place on Earth will surely change.

These sacred sites around the world will one day open up again as portals that signal to the demi-gods that another phase of humanity is about to begin. Until then, let's continue this amazing adventure!

End Notes

[1] Cunliffe, Barry and Colin Renfrew, eds. *Science and Stonehenge: Proceedings of The British Academy*. London: British Academy, 1997, page 1.

[2] Morgan, James; Tim Darvill and Geoff Wainwright, 21 September 2008. "*Dig pinpoints Stonehenge origins.*" BBC. Retrieved 22 September 2008.

[3] Schmid, Randolph E. 29 May 2008. "*Study: Stonehenge was a burial site for centuries.*" Associated Press. Archived from the original on 2008-06-01. Retrieved 29 May 2008.

[4] Cunliffe, Barry and Colin Renfrew. *Science and Stonehenge: Proceedings of The British Academy.* London: British Academy, 1997, page 8, para. 5.

[5] Atkinson, R. *Stonehenge*. London: Pelican Books, an imprint of Penguin, 1960, 165–6.

[6] Johnson, Anthony. *Solving Stonehenge*. London: Thames & Hudson, 2008.

[7] http://www.livescience.com/27832-strange-theories-about-stonehenge.html

[8] From a letter published in The Malta Independent, Monday, 7 October 2002, p.8, by Joseph Ellul, author of *The Hagar Qim Complex.*

[9] *In Places of Peace and Power: Temples of Neolithic Malta* (https://sacredsites.com/europe/malta/temples_malta.html).

[10] *In Mission Malta: Exploring the Sound and Energy Properties of Ancient Architecture* (https://grahamhancock.com/kreisbergg6).

Further Reading

Cunliffe, Barry and Colin Renfrew. *Science and Stonehenge: Proceedings of The British Academy*. London: The British Academy, 1997.

Foerster, Brian. *The Enigma of Tiwanaku and Puma Punku: A Visitor's Guide*. CreateSpace Independent Publishing Platform, 2015.

Grace, Sonja. *Become an Earth Angel: Advice and Wisdom for Finding Your Wings and Living in Service*. Scotland: Findhorn Press, 2014.

Hancock, Graham. *Magicians of the Gods: The Forgotten Wisdom of Earth's Lost Civilization*. New York, NY: Thomas Dunne Books, an imprint of St. Martin's Press, 2015.

Johnson, Anthony. *Solving Stonehenge: The New Key to an Ancient Enigma*. London: Thames & Hudson, 2008.

Lavelle, Des. *The Skellig Story: Ancient Monastic Outpost*. Dublin: O'Brien Press, 2004.

Shaffer, John A. *Winifred's Well*. Nashville, TN: Cold Tree Press, 2008.

Zamit, Prof. Sir Them. *The Copper Age Temples of Hagar Qim and Mnajdra*. Lija, Malta: Alpaprint, 1970.

About the Author

Sonja Grace is an internationally known mystic and healer, whose work helps people who suffer physically, mentally, emotionally, and spiritually. She is an energy surgeon who spirit-travels in order to work with her clients wherever they are in the world; she performs all levels of healing, including restructuring tissue and repairing organs, bones, blood, and cells. Sonja's ancestral background is a fascinating blend of Native American and Norwegian. She has been adopted by the Hopi Tribe of Arizona, where she is considered a medicine woman. Sonja is the author of *Become an Earth Angel* (Findhorn Press, 2014) and has appeared on *Beyond Belief* with George Noory, Coast to Coast AM, Better TV, AM Northwest, and the Virtual Light Broadcast. For more about Sonja Grace, go to www.sonjagrace.com

Also by Sonja Grace

Sonja Grace brings an entirely new perspective to the angel genre. She has been traveling and working in the angelic realm for over 30 years, is dedicated to Divine love and is an Earth Angel. Our planet has moved into the fifth dimension and we are about to witness a new order of earth angels. Hundreds of thousands of people are beginning to feel a calling to their spiritual light. Yet, some feel misunderstood, different and in many cases extremely sensitive and intuitive about people and events. Through her own extraordinary case studies, Sonja Grace reveals what it is like to do the work of an earth angel and how she has used her gifts to locate missing people, conduct long distance healing and council a myriad of international clients. Readers are taken on a journey into the angelic realms. Sonja Grace offers fresh insight and descriptions along with explanations of the angels and the earth angel phenomenon; what they are, how to identify them, what they do, where they come from and their particular mission at this time in the earth's history.

ISBN 978-1-84409-645-9

F I N D H O R N   P R E S S

Life-Changing Books

Consult our catalogue online
(with secure order facility) on
www.findhornpress.com

For information on the Findhorn Foundation:
www.findhorn.org